FLASHBACKS OF ABUSE

how a machine gun toting sociopath
freed me from the chains of my childhood

MARK DOUGLASS

Andover,
Minnesota

Publisher's Cataloging-In-Publication Data

Douglass, Mark.
Flashbacks of abuse : how a machine gun toting sociopath freed me from the chains of my childhood / Mark Douglass.

p. ; cm.

Cover title: Flashbacks of abuse
ISBN: 978-1-931945-81-3
ISBN: 1-931945-81-0

1. Douglass, Mark. 2. Adult child sexual abuse victims—Minnesota—Biography. 3. Male child sexual abuse victims—Minnesota—Biography. 4. Post-traumatic stress disorder—Patients—Minnesota—Biography. 5. Boys—Abuse of—Psychological aspects. 6. Victims of crimes—Psychology. I. Title. II. Title: Flashbacks of abuse

HV6570.2 .D68 2007
362.76/4/092 2007935692

Printed in the United States of America

First Printing: October 2007

11 10 09 08 07 5 4 3 2 1

Andover, Minnesota

Expert Publishing, Inc.
14314 Thrush Street NW,
Andover, MN 55304-3330
1-877-755-4966
www.expertpublishinginc.com

CONTENTS

	Acknowledgments	v
	Introduction	vii
ONE	*Baptism of Fire*	1
TWO	*Family Issues*	13
THREE	*Memories*	21
FOUR	*Realizing Who's Dangerous*	29
FIVE	*A Pre-teen Boy's Troubles*	35
SIX	*The Serpent Appears*	43
SEVEN	*Divide and Conquer*	47
EIGHT	*Isolation and Interrogation*	53
NINE	*Trained to Be Silent*	59
TEN	*The Nature of the Beast*	67
ELEVEN	*One Brick at a Time*	77
TWELVE	*The Blinders Come Off*	87
THIRTEEN	*I Had Enough*	97
FOURTEEN	*Metamorphosis*	103
FIFTEEN	*My Emerging Identity*	111
SIXTEEN	*Wedding*	117
SEVENTEEN	*Cleansing*	123
EIGHTEEN	*Trial and Judgment*	129
NINETEEN	*Harsh Reality*	133
TWENTY	*The Source of Happiness*	137
	Epilogue	141

ACKNOWLEDGMENTS

Although I owe thanks to many more people than I can name here, I acknowledge the contributions of the following:

My parents, who gave me life, who did the best they could in rearing me, and whom I love and also forgive, despite their all too human failings.

My childhood friend David's parents, Frank and Lee Roubik, whose friendship and guidance have meant so much to me over the years.

My many public school teachers, including Louis Duckett, Marilyn Rosien, Joan Bradach, and Charlotte Westby.

My college teachers, including James C. Turner, Ph.D., and Robert J. Kamilli, Ph.D.

Robert Jay Ginn, Jr., M.Div., career counselor, athletic advisor, and friend at Harvard.

My college friends, including Richard C. Norton, Jr., Malcolm and Amy Friedman, Charles and Shawna Wisnioski, Timothy Solberg, H. Scott Shore, and Elizabeth A. Bancroft, whose friendship sustained me.

My law school friends, including Paul Efros, Robert Schwartz, Mary Stone, and Martin Fox.

John A. Sweetser III, a mentor, friend, and father figure to me.

Hamline University School of Law Professor Richard T. Oakes and his wife, Carolyn, who patiently helped me and stood by me through many trying years during law school and my years as a practicing attorney.

Joseph G. Beaton, Jr., an attorney and colleague who had faith in my abilities as a lawyer, even when I lacked faith in myself.

Walter H. Rockenstein II, an attorney, mentor, and friend.

My law school classmate and attorney, James W. Kerr, and his former law firm partners: Steve Bergeson, Michael Lander, and Michael McDonald, who represented me in my legal case against Steve, when much of Minnesota statutes and case law were arrayed against me.

My many therapists and counselors, John A. Austin, Ph.D., Jayson Bischoff and Jack Tharp, Jeffrey R. Penn, M.D., Mic Hunter, Psy.D., and Dennis Conroy, Ph.D.

Peggy L. McNamara and other professional speakers at the Minnesota Chapter of the National Speakers Association, as well as Harry and Sharron Stockhausen, my publishers and editors at Expert Publishing, Inc.

My wife, Ann, who has inspired me and kept me alive with her love and devotion through more than a quarter century of marriage.

Our children, who have inspired and challenged me, who I hope will understand I did the best I could in rearing them, and who I hope will love and also forgive me for my all too human failings.

INTRODUCTION

In the last twenty years, or so, the phenomenon of male sexual abuse has moved from society's shadows out into the open. Where once medical, psychological, and law enforcement officials thought it to be a very minor problem affecting only a few boys and men, we now realize how tragically widespread the problem is.

Beginning in early childhood, men are told, "Big boys don't cry!" Men receive repeated messages and encouragement to "suck it up" and to not show emotion in the face of pain or disappointment. Men also do not reach out for help to family and friends as easily as women do. Men are terribly isolated from those around them. They are especially isolated from other men.

Many myths surrounding male sexual abuse further isolate men from themselves, one another, their families, and society. Consequently, men experience incredible emotional and psychological pain. Many men, particularly those who have been sexually abused as children, are shackled in the solitary confinement of debilitating shame. As a society, we see the consequences in their anger, depression, and their addictions to alcohol, drugs, sex, gambling, work, risk, and crime. These and other issues hide the true problem from society. The core issue, male sexual abuse, remains hidden and untreated for too many boys and men.

I was a childhood victim of sexual abuse at the hands of a close family friend. This sociopathic predator first assaulted me when I was a pubescent twelve-year-old boy. I was at a critical juncture in my psychological and emotional development into a young man. That normal development, in some ways, was stunted by the abuse. The sexual assaults, emotional domination, and the manipulations of the close family friend led to my psychological and emotional isolation from family, friends, and society. In shame, I kept silent about my childhood sexual abuse from age twelve until my early thirties. I then began a journey of struggle and discovery as I attempted to free my imprisoned childhood self.

In 2004, while traveling in Europe, my twelve-year-old daughter and I were almost killed while accidentally stumbling into the middle of a gangland kidnapping. This narrow brush with death, coupled with my growing awareness of my own mortality, inadvertently proved to be a gift of immense value.

This book is the story of my journey of recovery away from the ravages of childhood sexual abuse and its isolation, back to health and back into society at large.

CHAPTER ONE

Baptism of Fire

As we walked past a nineteenth century mansion at 45 Roemer Visscherstraat, we heard the first of five or six shots from a .45 caliber Thompson sub-machine gun—the kind U.S. Army paratroopers used during World War II. The very loud "BAM" came from only thirty yards behind us. My twelve-year-old daughter and I looked over our shoulders and turned around to see two swarthy men dressed in black leather jackets running towards us. The man closest to us looked absolutely terrified. The gunman followed, only five or ten yards behind him, firing his gun in single shots—not in the fully automatic mode—the rat-a-tat-tat manner of which it was capable. The first man zigged and zagged, left then right, in an attempt to elude his predator. The prey looked up the street towards us and, I think, realized we were in danger of being killed depending upon where he ran. Rather than running up the broad sidewalk upon which we were standing, he darted into the middle of the street. But we stood on the corner of a slight bend in the street. In order to get and keep the furthest distance from the gunman, the victim had to cut that corner, while still running in the street. At the closest point, only a parked car, plus a couple feet either side of it, separated the victim, and a moment later, the gunman, from us. My daughter and I were witnessing a gangland kidnapping.

A minute or two before we heard the first gunshot, my daughter and I stood by a park bench only a few yards away from Amsterdam Film Museum overlooking the Vondelpark, a large central park. I had pulled out my pocket map, opened it up, and sought my bearings. I wanted to make our way to the Van Gogh Museum several blocks away. As I looked at the map, I saw we could follow the park's walking path straight ahead some distance until it intersected a busy street that would take us to the museum. But just ahead on that path were five or six dark-haired men, Mediterranean men—Greek, Italian, Spanish, or perhaps Middle Eastern. All had dark clothing; several wore black leather jackets or sports coats. They stood in the middle of the path in front of another park bench. They talked intensely with one another. To the left of the footpath was a large wrought iron gate through which horse-drawn carriages once passed in an earlier, more elegant era, but now served as a pedestrian entrance to the Vondelpark. This gate opened onto a one-block-long street, which led to the same busy street that would take us to the Van Gogh Museum. For some unknown reason, I decided my daughter and I should avoid the group of men blocking the footpath. Instead, we went through the large, old, carriage gate to Roemer Visscherstraat. Thus, in seeking to avoid trouble, while we vacationed in the Netherlands, my decision guaranteed our encounter with it.

In the aftermath of a dramatic and life-threatening event, you often look back upon your day with wonder. What if you had stopped for coffee and tarried a bit? What if you had turned left along your route, instead of going right? What if you had simply slept a little later that day? My daughter and I awakened that morning in March of 2004 in a cramped hotel room overlooking the town square of the rather sleepy town of Haarlem. It was only a twenty-minute train ride away from Amsterdam. The pace there was more subdued. The accommodations were cheaper. We dressed, locked up the room, and took the two-person elevator, which was the size of a small clothes closet, down to the hotel's modest main salon where we dined on the complimentary continental breakfast offered to hotel guests. We then hurried down the hill several blocks to the train station. I was on a mission.

My daughter was a sixth grader at the time of this vacation. Her middle school English teacher assigned the *Diary of a Young Girl* by Anne Frank. I itched to, once again, travel in Europe. I also had about three thousand dollars sitting in my bank account, which was begging to be spent. I proposed to my daughter that we go to Amsterdam to visit the house where Anne Frank, her family, and a few other Jews hid out during World War II in an attempt to avoid capture by the Nazis and certain death in their concentration camps. Most Amsterdam travel guidebooks warn long lines awaited every tourist visiting the Anne Frank Museum. To avoid the lines one must arrive very early, or very late, in the day. Failing this, one was likely to face waiting lines, which, in peak travel season, often snaked around the corner and up the block. I have little patience for lines of people and the discomfort of crowds. We hurried along in our itinerary arriving just after the museum opened its doors.

We took an hour or so to tour the museum. Afterwards, just before noon, we had a snack in the museum's second floor coffee shop. As we enjoyed our snack we discussed Anne Frank and what we had seen in the museum. We looked out through the coffee shop windows. As expected, the tourist line stretched around the corner and well up the street. The guidebooks were right. I remember thinking to myself, and remarking to my daughter, how wonderfully clever we were to beat the rush. Looking back on things, those tourists waiting in that line did not have an appointment with destiny as my daughter and I had. Our appointment was only an hour or so away.

After visiting the Anne Frank Museum, we wandered about looking at the old houses, the people, and the canals as we tried to avoid being run over by bicyclists or motorists. My daughter, like so many girls at a preteen stage of life, loved everything about horses. Looking in the Amsterdam tourist guidebook, I saw the Hollandsche Manege, the Dutch riding school, lay within walking distance. So, as we walked and talked and looked at the scenery, I guided us towards the riding school. I had the vague hope the riding school would, for a fee, let my daughter ride in the equestrian arena for an hour. Meandering here and there, we found the riding school, entered it, and watched a Dutch riding instructor give dressage lessons to a young patrician woman beautifully attired in formal riding gear sitting atop her handsome mount. This was far from my expectation. It was obvious to me, my daughter would not be renting a horse that day. We watched the riding lesson for five or ten minutes. My daughter kept nudging me and telling me we really needed to leave. She felt out of place in this equestrian establishment. She had seen an impatiently worded sign to English-speaking visitors that said, in essence, unless you spoke fluent Dutch enough to read and understand all the rules posted about the stables, you were in the wrong place. I wanted to tarry. My daughter wanted to leave. So leave we did. Our appointment loomed ever closer.

We walked out of the riding school, down the street, around one side of a small church, and along the the northern edge of the Vondelpark, a large central park located in what was once an upper class neighborhood filled with lovely townhouses. We walked along the path until we stood in front of a former mansion that now housed the Film Museum, a classic film venue.

Over the years, when our family traveled, we learned a trip should not include things of interest only to my wife and me. Nor should it be entirely focused on the children's interests. We learned to keep our respective sanities by including something for the adults and something for the children. In traveling to the Netherlands with my daughter, I wanted her to see the Anne Frank Museum. I wanted her to see and experience many things Dutch. Among these things, I wanted to see the Van Gogh Museum and also some museums exhibiting the Old Masters such as Rembrandt, Vermeer, Van Eyck, and Hals.

So there we were, having seen two places of interest to my daughter, the Anne Frank Museum and the Hollandsche Manege riding school. I now looked forward to, and I charted our course from, the Vondelpark to the Van Gogh Museum several blocks away. I did not plan for our appointment with destiny on Roemer Visscherstraat a little after 1:00 p.m. I did not plan for the life threatening, and ultimately, life altering drama that awaited us on our first full day of vacation.

The first gunshot loudly commanded our undivided attention. We looked over our shoulders and then turned to face the unfolding drama. The four or five shots afterwards sounded like shots fired from a children's cap gun having strangely muffled reports. We stood in shock with our mouths agape for about twenty or thirty seconds until the men were abreast of us. In this period of shock, numerous things happened to me, my thinking, and my perceptions. First, my vision telescoped down to focus upon the two men. All things peripheral disappeared. Time slowed to a glacial pace, but numerous thoughts raced through my mind. The first man did not appear to be a savory character to me. I assumed he was a criminal. I assumed the gunman was an undercover policeman by engaging in the following thought process. *We are in the Netherlands, which has some of the world's strictest gun control laws. It is illegal for a private party to own a gun in the Netherlands. The gunman possesses a machine gun. He is chasing what appears to be a criminal. The gunman must be a policeman. Since he is not in uniform, he must be an undercover policeman. Since he is a policeman, my daughter and I are safe.* We stood motionless.

The muffled gunshots were particularly disturbing to me. I have owned firearms since I was a teenager. (If you include a BB gun with those, I have owned a gun since I was eight years old.) Most guns are so loud, repeated firing of them without using ear protection will result in pain and, over time, deafness. The only time I have fired a gun and have not noticed the loudness of its report was when I was hunting. At those times when you are preoccupied with shooting your prey, you hardly notice the sound of your own rifle or shotgun because of your intense concentration. During the twenty or thirty seconds in Amsterdam, I forgot this fact. I was tremendously puzzled with why the machine gun's report was so quiet. Familiar as I was with guns, I looked at the machine gun and did not see a silencer attached to it.

Also in the course of pursuing and firing at his prey, I could not understand why the gunman's bullets failed to strike him. The last shot I heard sounded like a splat. I thought certainly the gunman must have struck the fleeing criminal, the sound being the bullet striking the man's black leather jacket and his flesh beneath. But the fleeing criminal did not falter or fall. (What I learned weeks after the incident was the "splat" sound was a bullet striking the car next to which I was standing. The bullet missed me by three feet or less.)

About this time, a light colored Volkswagen Golf sped up the street from the Vondelpark, passed the unfolding drama, turned on the busy street, and disappeared. We learned later that while the gunman chased his prey before us, his accomplices spirited away his prey's twin brother to be held for ransom. These were the other men we had seen in the Vondelpark.

As the two men ran abreast of us, separated from us by one car's width, I began to think there might be some danger to my daughter and me. I imagined the *criminal* might, at any moment, pull a pistol out of his pocket, turn on his heel, and return fire at the *policeman*, but in our direction. I yelled to my daughter, "Get down!" while pushing her down and maneuvering her across the wide sidewalk to the base of a mansion's front steps. I then carefully covered my daughter's torso and head with my body in my attempt to protect her from harm. We lay there for another thirty seconds or so.

The gunman, whom I imagined to be a policeman, returned and stood about five or six feet from us. Since I was facing down, I could only hear him. My daughter was on the sidewalk, lying on her back and facing up. She saw the gunman and his actions. The gunman paused for a moment, perhaps thinking of his own daughter or his own niece. Apparently observing our manner of dress, and also having, moments earlier, heard me command my daughter to get down, the gunman commanded us, in English, "Stay down." Thinking he was a policeman, I replied, "Yes!"

Continuing to think he was a policeman, as he ran off, I expected a team of policemen to arrive shortly at the scene to check on our well-being. The time passed. No policemen arrived. As I lay next to and atop my daughter, she innocently asked, "Dad, what just happened?" Pondering the question, I replied with growing fear and uncertainty, "Either a bad guy was chasing a bad guy, or a policeman was chasing a bad guy. But I don't know which." Thinking some more, I suddenly felt terribly vulnerable about our situation. I thought we would be safer if we swiftly departed for the Van Gogh Museum. I said to my daughter, "We are not going to wait around to find an answer to your question."

We stood up and scurried off to the Van Gogh Museum. My daughter commented further, "Well, at least it wasn't one of those drive-by shootings we hear about on TV and in school." I said, "No. At least it wasn't a *drive-by* shooting." I thought to myself, "It was a *run-by* shooting!"

As we quickly walked along the busy street leading to the Van Gogh Museum, we heard the distinctive European police car siren of the first officers to respond to reports of gunfire—"DEE—dah, DEE—dah, DEE—dah." Finally realizing we had just had an encounter with near-death, I immediately burst into tears. Somehow, I felt ashamed, and had to turn away from my daughter as I began to sob. Then, almost immediately I willed myself to get a grip. We continued the next few blocks to the Van Gogh Museum. Having witnessed this life-threatening drama on an isolated city street, I suddenly needed the security of a crowd. We reached the museum, paid for our tickets, and sought its much-welcomed refuge.

However, the refuge couldn't shelter me from the tidal wave of terror and paranoia rising within me. I mustered all my strength to stay in control as I pondered what was to be done. So many questions filled my mind, each demanding priority.

What happened? Why did I misread the event so badly? Why was I immobilized during the first moments of shooting? Why didn't I feel any fear until several minutes afterwards? Why did the gunshots sound so muffled? Why did my field of vision telescope to see only the two men and the gun, largely to the exclusion of houses, wrought iron fences, street lamps, window boxes, and other details I would have observed and absorbed in more tranquil circumstances?

As a lawyer, I struggled with the issue of duty. Did we owe a duty to this foreign country to step forward and give our accounts to the police? Did we owe a duty to society at large? Did we owe a duty to do our part to fight evil? Did we owe a duty to ourselves? Ultimately, could I live with myself as a lawyer and a believer in law and order if we just walked away from the whole thing? If we gave statements to the police, just what details could we provide to help the police? The submachine gun remained clearer to me than any identifying details of the victim or the gunman.

As a father, I wondered about other questions. If we identified ourselves as witnesses, would we be detained? Would our identities and our address back home be revealed to the gunman and his confederates through their attorneys? What kind of parental modeling should I exhibit? Do I want my child to be civic minded and a responsible citizen? More pointedly, if I was willing to take risks by talking to the police, was it fair to subject my daughter, and my family back home, to the same risks? How could I keep my child safe from further harm? What kind of father am I?

As a survivor of childhood sexual abuse, other issues arose. Could we trust the police and the Dutch legal system? Could their promises of confidentiality be believed? What safeguards did their laws provide us from being threatened or killed so a gangland criminal will get off scot-free? Could I forgive myself for *not* behaving and acting like a Hollywood action hero? I was in severe emotional and intellectual pain. What kind of man was I?

The street drama's span of a minute or two, compounded by so many questions arising from it, upended my entire life.

My daughter and I spent about an hour looking at a tremendous array of paintings and drawings by Vincent Van Gogh. One of the prime reasons for our coming to the Netherlands—to Amsterdam—was so I could see these masterpieces, so my artistic daughter could see these masterpieces. The entire time we were in the museum's quiet safety, my mind tried to answer all the questions coursing through it. My mind tried to answer many—should have, could have, would have—questions. As we walked out of the museum, I realized I looked at, but had not seen, one single painting or drawing in that building. However, I answered one of my questions. I turned to my daughter and said, "We have to find a police officer and tell him what we saw. If we cannot find one near, we have to go back to the scene of the shooting." In the next five or ten minutes the old joke, "You can never find a policeman when you need one!" held new meaning for me. Finding no policeman, I told my daughter, "Okay. We must go back."

A few minutes later, we arrived at the crime scene to see police barricades blocking both ends of the street. Crowds of onlookers politely stood back from the yellow plastic tape strung out in front of us. Within the cordoned off zone, dozens of police officers, forensic investigators, dog handlers, and photographers were combing the scene for evidence. They located each rifle slug and each spent brass shell casing. These were marked with an identifying number awaiting the appropriate person to map it, photograph it, and secure it for evidentiary purposes.

I spotted a woman officer who appeared to be in charge. I yelled, "Agent," the Dutch word for police officer, but pronounced "Ahh-Ghent." She came over to me and began speaking to me in English. I informed her what my daughter and I had seen. A newspaper reporter sidled up to me and exhorted me, also in English, to tell my story to the world. Having had my words misrepresented a few times over the years by journalists, I declined. The lawyer in me also knew not to give multiple statements about any matter. There would inevitably be inconsistencies. A future defense attorney could destroy me and my credibility if the matter went to court. The agent advised me not to talk to anyone about the matter. I told her, "The journalist over there wants me to talk with her so she can write a story." The agent looked at the reporter whom she recognized, then the agent looked back at me and said, "Don't talk to anyone, *especially* her."

My God! It then dawned on me, I just announced to the crowd surrounding me and my daughter we were material witnesses. It further dawned on me, the gunman or his associate may be present within the crowd. Trembling with this realization, I crossed under the police barricades to pursue the agent as she returned to her duties. Fearing my contaminating the crime scene, she ordered me back behind the lines. I told her my daughter and I wanted to be taken from the scene—and the crowds—immediately. She obliged me. We were placed in a police cruiser with the only other witness, a Dutchwoman. We were then whisked across town to the sound of the police cruiser's wailing siren. They delivered the Dutchwoman to one police station. My daughter and I were taken to another where we awaited an off-duty detective who was fluent in English to arrive.

The English-speaking detective finally arrived and interviewed us for much of the afternoon. We described what we heard and saw, but only after I was thoroughly assured our names and addresses would not be released to the criminals or their defense attorneys. I described, in detail, the submachine gun and even drew a picture of it. I explained what I could about the victim and the gunman, but because of my obsession with the gun and its muffled reports, I could not describe them in enough detail for me to make an identification in a police line-up. Of course, my daughter observed some things I did not. While she was making her statement, she described how the gunman's submachine gun had jammed. She further explained that while standing over us, he cleared a spent shell casing from the gun's action, and rammed the bolt closed, thus placing a new bullet into the gun's chamber. Hearing this, I grasped the devastating understanding of how our lives and our fates had hung in the balance, completely dependent upon the charity of a sociopath. What prevented him from executing us, then and there, as inconvenient witnesses?

When we finished the interview and submitted witness statements, the detective drove us to the nearest tram stop, thanked us, and gave us instructions on which tram to take to the city center so we could transfer to a train back to Haarlem. It was late in the afternoon. People were returning home from work. The Haarlem train was very crowded—standing room only. As I looked about the train compartment, I noticed several commuters who appeared to be Mediterranean. I focused on one man. My gaze kept returning to him. He caught my eye, and his gaze kept coming back to me. At that moment, I feared he was an assassin who was going to kill us! Terror welled up within me. At Haarlem, we quickly exited the train. I kept a watch all about me. As we walked from the train station to our hotel, I looked over my shoulder, always checking to see if we were being tailed. My daughter asked with a teenaged mixture of annoyance and concern, "Dad, why do you keep looking over your shoulder?" I confessed to her I was afraid. I feared friends of the gunman might be following us. Of course, they had not. The day's misadventure made me hyper-vigilant. All my adult life, probably a result of my childhood sexual abuse, I have been vigilant when outside my home. In the days following the shooting incident, and for months after our return to the U.S., hyper-vigilance was my constant companion.

That night, I wrote in my travel journal about our experience. I barely slept. I cried a lot. If I ever felt safe in this world, I certainly no longer did. In an effort to deal with the event, and inform but not scare my wife, I wrote a flippant e-mail to my wife about how our daughter and I spent much of the first full vacation day in a Netherlands police station giving our accounts of the incident—"Having a good time, wish you were here!"

Apart from the hyper-vigilance, the most disturbing thing happened when I later recounted to others what had happened. They politely listened, but their faces contorted into expressions of incredible discomfort and horror. This routine, almost guaranteed, response trained me to not tell people about the matter. This isolated me from the world precisely when I needed to reconnect with it. I also realized most people live in a comfortable self-satisfied bubble that they believe will never burst. They may read terrible things in the newspaper or see terrible things on TV, but their day-to-day worlds feel safe and comfy. My story threatened their bubbles of denial.

My daughter and I somehow enjoyed the remainder of our vacation. But, we carried around some extra baggage. For me, the shooting kept playing and replaying in my mind like a movie. The movie was a double feature. The second show contained an amazing variety of scenarios wherein I single-handedly fought and captured the armed gunman in the manner of a silver-screen hero. I worked through these scenarios endlessly. No matter what scenario ran through my mind, each involved risk to my daughter's health or life. Certainly, each scenario involved the possibility of my injury or death. The movie played almost every waking minute of our holiday. Its long run lasted for days, weeks, and months after our return home.

I needed help. I suffered from post traumatic stress disorder (PTSD). After returning home, I called my wife's friend who works in law enforcement. She suggested I talk with a retired police officer who now practiced as a psychologist. It turned out to be a perfect referral. He had counseled many police officers over the years who had survived shooting incidents while in the line of duty. This therapist had even been involved in shooting incidents, or other critical incidents, during his years on the police force. It was clear to me from his personal and professional experience, this man understood what tormented me.

A severely traumatic event can unearth many feelings and issues from past life events. My case was no different. The Vondelpark shooting incident unearthed many issues from my past as a childhood sexual abuse victim at the hands of a close family friend Steve. The parallels soon became evident. In Amsterdam, in the course of only a few minutes, a powerful sociopath barged into my life. My daughter and I were largely helpless to do anything in the face of his submachine gun and his willingness to use it. Here at home, over the course of several years, a powerful sociopath wheedled his way into my teenaged life. As a child, I was helpless to do anything in the face of his adult sophistication, manipulations, and his complete disregard for my well-being.

In Amsterdam, as a father, I faced evil forces from which I needed to protect my daughter. Here at home, forty years earlier, my parents faced an evil man from which I needed their protection. In one case the child was protected by the parent. In the earlier case, the child was not protected.

In both cases, the sociopaths deeply wounded those around them, not by death or physical injury—but by the *threat* of death or physical injury. Both cases left psychological wounds. In 2004 in Amsterdam, on the edge of the Vondelpark, on a quiet residential street, the wounds inflicted by the machine gun toting sociopath inadvertently led to the eventual healing of very old wounds in me, wounds I first received in 1963 when I was twelve years old.

CHAPTER TWO

Family Issues

It was as if forty years of my life were arrayed upon a bookshelf like a set of encyclopedias. The first volume of the set was Steve, the close family friend and sociopath. The last volume was an unknown sociopathic gunman spraying bullets about an otherwise quiet street in Amsterdam, threatening my daughter's and my life. This life and these books were set between bookends made of post traumatic stress disorder (PTSD)—my father's at one end, and mine at the other end. The more distant PTSD in my life, my father's, arose from his wartime experiences. As distant as his PTSD was from my present circumstances, it, nevertheless, affected me during my childhood. Because of the shooting incident in Amsterdam, I now endured PTSD in the hours, days, weeks, and months following our vacation.

My father piloted a B-17 bomber during World War II. In 1943, during the early months of the American Eighth Air Force's air war over Europe, my father's bombardment group was stationed in England. After two years of training in the United States, the group's very first mission was to bomb an automotive factory in Belgium. On this mission, my father's B-17 was shot down by the Germans. He and his crew bailed out over the Dutch-Belgian border. My father landed near Terneuzen, the Netherlands.

Mark Twain once observed, "History doesn't repeat itself, but it does rhyme." The rhyme in the verses of my life was my father's PTSD and my own, both of which began in the land of wooden shoes and windmills.

What a strong dose of reality it must have been for my father and his crew, after training together for so many months prior. Moments after the bombardier released the aircraft's bomb load, two of my father's crew members were wounded by a burst of flak that came up through the open bomb bay doors. Had the flak exploded only seconds before, the bombs would have still been inside the aircraft, loaded in their racks. The flak would have ignited the bombs. My father and his crew would have been pulverized by their massive explosion. There would have been no survivors. My oldest brother would have lost his father and my mother widowed. My other brother, my younger sister, and I would never have been conceived. We never would have experienced the wonders of this life.

It is amazing to me how just a few seconds affected the fate of my father and his crew. By comparison, just a minute's time difference in my daughter's and my walk along the edge of Amsterdam's Vondelpark would have spared us from being witnesses and victims of a violent crime.

During my father's mission, enemy fire struck one of the B-17's engines. The engine fire, ignited by enemy gunfire or flak, could not be extinguished. As his plane fell behind and dropped out of flight formation, my father knew from his pilot training one of two things was likely. Either the engine would melt its wing mountings, break loose from the wing, and send the plane into an uncontrolled dive, or enemy fighters would finish his plane off. In either case, my father's B-17 was very likely headed for a crash, taking him and his crew to their deaths unless they could parachute to safety. My father ordered his crew members to jump, while he tried to keep the aircraft's flight steady. When it was his turn to jump, he reached under his seat to get his parachute. It was gone! Just then, the aircraft went into the expected steep dive. The G-forces upon my father prevented him from moving. Yet, he now saw his parachute right in front of him, just beyond his reach.

Seemingly, he was doomed. Just as my father had all but given up, he prayed. Providentially, after such a steep and lengthy descent, my father's B-17 momentarily pulled out of its dive and leveled off at an altitude of less than 1,000 feet. My father was able to put on his parachute, and get out of the doomed aircraft, with only seconds to spare. So close to the ground, he did not bother to count the usual "one-one-thousand, two-one-thousand—up to ten-one-thousand" to be certain he cleared the aircraft. Instead, he almost immediately pulled his ripcord to open his parachute. Like a pendulum, he swung only twice, and then he struck the ground—alive. As he gathered up his parachute, he was immediately captured by two German soldiers. While aiming their rifles at my father, his captors demanded firmly, but politely in German, "Ihre Pistole, bitte." My father surrendered his .45 caliber side arm to them. As they took him away to captivity, in halting, heavily accented English, they offered the oft-repeated judgment given so many Allied airmen, "For Yuu, ze Vahr ist oh-fer."

My father spent the remaining twenty-two months of the war as a prisoner of war. Most of his imprisonment was in the POW camp known as Stalag Luft III, where he helped dig the tunnel through which seventy-six prisoners escaped, as chronicled in the book and the movie, *The Great Escape*. In January 1945, as the Russian armies advanced from the East, the more than 10,000 Allied officers imprisoned at Stalag Luft III were force-marched through bitter cold and blizzard conditions, then packed into cattle cars, and transported to POW camps in western Germany. In April 1945, Patton's Third Army liberated my father and thousands of other POWs from my father's new camp, Stalag Luft VII-A in Moosburg, Germany. Less than a month later, the war in Europe was over.

My father and his comrades, having lived on greatly reduced rations for so many months, were too emaciated and sickly to return immediately home to the U.S. Instead, he spent a month or so at one of several Allied rehabilitation camps for ex-POWs named after popular cigarette brands. My father, a lifelong lover of Lucky Strike cigarettes, was sent, appropriately enough, to Camp Lucky Strike in northern France, where he was given clean clothes and was fed all the food he could eat. He then returned to Minnesota by troop ship to Boston, and by railroad to Minneapolis.

How odd it must have been for him to come home. How joyous, but also strange to see his parents and his sister again. How awkward to become reacquainted with his wife, and to meet his three-year-old son, whom he had last seen as a mere infant.

My father, like so many other combat veterans, talked little about his wartime experiences. How do you talk about combat, its exhilaration, your fears, injury, death, and imprisonment when these experiences are so outside of the normal day-to-day life of your loved ones? Who could understand these things, but another combat veteran? Who would want to forget their experience, but a combat veteran—so they could just get on with the business of living? It must have been hard for my father to keep the emotional and psychological lid on. Cracking the lid just a little bit risked letting it all out in an emotional breakdown. Breaking down might mean you were something less than a man. Yet, sometimes, when I was a child, as he tucked me into bed at night, I was able get him to tell me about the war. He obliged me with a sanitized recollection of events. The *facts*, but not the *emotions*. When I was older, if I asked more probing questions of his bombing mission and his imprisonment, he deflected the conversation to other, less troubling, topics apart from the war. Throughout my childhood, my father's emotional lid stayed on tight. I think that by keeping it on tight my father found it difficult to deal with the demands of fatherhood. Yet, he couldn't stand any level of chaos or struggle. What is child-rearing but chaos and struggle?

He needed to be alone from time to time. I think depression dogged him repeatedly. I know he didn't like being in the midst of crowds. The houses we lived in never had fences around them. Having lived on starvation rations as a POW, after the war he preferred to eat several small meals each day rather than three large meals. We children were never allowed to decline the food we were served at family meals. To waste perfectly good food was sacrilegious. When I was a child, how declining Brussels sprouts or tunafish casserole was sinful, I never could understand!

My mother once remarked to me that prior to World War II, my father had been a handsome, charming, happy-go-lucky man who had not a care in the world. As a child and as a young man, he had been a brilliant student. Just about anything he decided to do, he did with great ease and perfection. He was a golden boy whose life showed great promise. In contrast, after the war, he was serious and had a no-nonsense, all-business approach to life. During the war, while in the Army Air Forces, he had been a gambler. On payday poker games, my father routinely routed the other, younger, greener, card players. My mother told me, in 1942 my father once came home to their off-base apartment with all of his pants and shirt pockets, as well as the inside of his shirt, stuffed with his gambling winnings from an evening of poker—over $5,000. (In 2007 dollars, this is the equivalent of over $60,000!) By comparison, when I was growing up, he would sometimes bet his fellow golf players for each hole in a round of golf. The limit was a quarter or fifty cents per hole. My mother told me that after the war, my father was strictly business, self-controlled, and unwilling to take major risks. Like so many other combat veterans, the war left deep marks upon him, maturing him, but also sobering him.

A returning combat veteran brings home his duffelbag filled with clothes and his shaving kit. He often brings home another *ephemeral* emotional and psychological bag that sits in the corner of the room, not to be opened, its content never to be aired out or laundered. However you label the contents of that bag the family is profoundly affected. I was affected. My father was distant. Perhaps had he not had his wartime experiences, he still would have been distant.

In many ways, I was very much like him. Sometimes, it is hardest to parent a child who is a mirror image of you. When the child embodies your positive traits, as well as your Jungian shadow, being a parent forces you to confront all the faults you would avoid seeing in yourself.

Whatever the reason, for many years I felt I could not bridge the gap between us, and, sadly, I felt I could never measure up to him as a man. Since my father was a highly disciplined and moral man, the shame and guilt later introduced into my life by Steve widened this gap and increased my feelings of inadequacy.

My father could not stand to engage in controversy or struggle. We children knew this. My mother's threats of "Wait until your father gets home!" had particular meaning. This meaning was not so much that he would come home, learn of our transgressions, and fly off the handle, causing us physical harm. Actually, my mother was more emotional, volatile, and uneven in her discipline of us children. My father, could be severe in his discipline, but it was measured, reasoned discipline. For me, "Wait until your father gets home!" had a secondary meaning. Whatever we did, we mustn't upset father. We must try to protect him.

Two incidents come to mind in which we sought to protect father. One happened when I was a child of eight or nine. The other occurred when I was about thirty.

My father smoked Lucky Strike cigarettes from the time he was a teenager until his death at age sixty-nine in 1985. He always hid his smoking from his parents, and from his mother, in particular. Smoking was one of the ways he rebelled against his mother, who was a perfectionist and a controlling parent. Yet, to openly acknowledge smoking to his mother was a level of defiance my father could not muster. It also was a matter of shame he could not face. Secondly, his addiction to nicotine, in his view, his mother's view, and his church's view, violated the first Biblical commandment—"Thou shalt have no other gods before me."

One time, grandmother and grandfather telephoned our home. They announced they were only minutes away and wanted to drop by to see us grandchildren. For the next twenty minutes, my mother and we children ran about the house, in a desperate, headlong effort, emptying ash trays, hiding ash trays, matches, cigarette packs, and opening windows to air the house out before our grandparents arrived. Thus, we were enlisted in protecting father.

As I look back over the years, there is no way this ruse could have fooled my grandmother. Our house must have reeked of tobacco smoke. By her silent acquiescence, even grandmother was enlisted in protecting my father. I suppose she was just saving face. By not stating the obvious, she allowed my father to save face also. I don't know if this was courtesy or co-dependence.

The second incident occurred when, in my late thirties, I first broke to my family the protracted silence about my sexual abuse. Several of us went to a joint counseling session with one of my first therapists. I was sitting between my wife and my father. My mother was sitting on the other side of my father. In the course of this family counseling session, I made a particularly difficult revelation about our family friend Steve, his conduct towards me, and the manner in which Steve had lied about everything to my parents. As I made this revelation, I reached over to soften the blow to my father by placing my hand upon his hand. In a peculiar way, our roles were reversed. I became the consoling father. My father was the saddened child. As I did this, my therapist's and a co-counselor's eyes zeroed in upon my comforting gesture to my father. Observing my co-therapists' facial tells, I shamefully realized how I had always sought to protect my father in his delicate condition. I realized we all had.

My father's vulnerability, arising from his wartime experiences and his own failure to resolve those issues, interfered with his ability to parent and protect us children. Because he hated struggle and situations that disturbed his own equilibrium—because he could not let the lid come off his own psychological turmoil, he hated dealing with the struggles of each of our teenaged years. His distance, coupled with my being too much trouble, was the perfect opportunity for a man like Steve.

To my father, and my mother, in response to my teenaged rebellion (made worse by Steve), Steve's assurances to them were a welcome balm. "Don't worry. I'll talk with the boy. I'll try to iron things out for you," Steve intoned.

To me, Steve would say, "Mark, your parents are so old-fashioned and unreasonable! I don't know how you put up with them. But don't worry. I'll talk with them. I'll try to iron things out for you."

Our family friend Steve had a knack for discovering exactly how our family and other families were unhappy. He then crafted his approach to exploit that unhappiness so he could divide the family and conquer its boys. After conquering me, Steve never thought I would one day rise up and be free of him.

CHAPTER THREE

Memories

Incredibly, when I look back upon my childhood family life, I want to idealize it. I want to think of it in terms of the television sitcoms of the day such as *Father Knows Best*, *The Donna Reed Show*, or *The Adventures of Ozzie and Harriet*. My parents worked hard. They were good citizens. They were good people. We children were well scrubbed and well fed. We lived in a spacious home in a nice neighborhood. My father worked five days a week, sometimes six, at his dental practice. He earned a good living, but he wasn't rich. We lived a good life, but it was by no means an extravagant one.

My father, a student of economic history and the stock market, always feared a recurrence of the Great Depression. He feared he wouldn't have enough dental patients, or that having enough, they would not be able to pay him for his work. He and my mother always worried about making ends meet. Because my parents grew up during the Great Depression of the 1930s, they knew the importance of budgeting their money, spending wisely, and making do with what you had until you could afford something better.

Long before it was popularized by the environmental movement, my parents seemed to have invented recycling. Their recycling was not the curbside variety whereby you separate glass, metal, paper, and plastic. Their recycling was to take something, use it, re-use, and re-use it again. For example, when my oldest brother, reached a certain age, say fifteen, he needed his first suit. My mother took my brother to the local department store during a sale. There they found an acceptable brown suit with stuffed shoulders and wide lapels. "You look quite handsome, son. This suit is just the ticket," she might have said to him.

When my oldest brother outgrew the suit, it passed on to a male cousin across town, who was about a year younger. When he outgrew it, it was passed back to my next oldest brother. After his use, the suit was passed back across town to the next male cousin in line. Then it bounced back to me. When, I was done with it, it went back across town yet another time, to be worn by my youngest two male cousins. Of course, by the time it reached the very youngest male cousin, the suit was a bit shiny in places, and it had been mended here and there. But the wide lapels and the over-stuffed shoulders, so in style when my oldest brother first wore it, were so out of style with the thin cut lapels and unpadded shoulders then in vogue.

My mother enjoyed recycling furniture. Except for a new television set, I don't recall my mother ever buying a new piece of furniture. Instead, she would go with a friend to a Salvation Army Thrift Store to buy a needed piece of furniture. Together, they would strip it of old paint and upholstery. They would repaint or restain it, and reupholster it. Their work breathed new life into some old, solid pieces of furniture, some of which are still in my home and my siblings' homes. But you didn't buy any more than you could afford. You didn't have credit cards to briefly satisfy your whims, while gently and permanently shackling you with high interest debt.

My mother and her friend applied the same principles to their houses. My mother, or her friend, decided a certain room in their respective houses needed to be redecorated. They worked as a team, stripping layer upon layer of paint, varnish, and wallpaper. They then re-did the room in a style more suited to their individual tastes. For every day my mother worked at her friend's house, her friend spent a day working at our house. Together, they created value for their families, while enjoying each other's company and cementing a lifelong friendship.

The 1950s and 1960s was *not* a fast-food era. People didn't defrost precooked meals and throw them in the microwave to heat them up. TV dinners had only been invented a few years before. Household microwave ovens were not widely available, even though microwave ovens had been demonstrated and first exhibited in the *kitchen of the future* at the 1939 World's Fair in New York.

Instead, my mother cooked a great deal of our meals from scratch. Sometimes, to save some time, she would make something like meatloaf using a can of Campbell's soup as part of the recipe. My mother was a virtuoso in extending and improvising a recipe with Campbell's soup and some noodles. One wonderful memory from my childhood was that she constantly baked delicious bread, pies, cakes, and caramel rolls.

Naturally, the demands of earning a living and raising a family led my parents to divide up various duties between them. Because this was the 1950s, father worked downtown and mother worked at home, taking care of us four children. My father ran his dental practice and attended to major disciplinary questions of our upbringing. My mother ran the household affairs and the moment-to-moment disciplining of us children. Their arrangements were not unusual for the times.

They were a good team. Together, they each had better lives than if they had lived apart. But, I think something was missing in their love for each other. There is an old joke about an old North Dakota farmer, who, having just buried his wife of fifty years, walked, contemplatively, with the minister from the cemetery back to the church and the funeral reception in the church basement. The minister asked the farmer, "With such an enduring marriage, you must have really loved your wife."

The farmer thought for a moment and said, "Reverend, I loved her so much—I almost told her."

Humor presents tragedy in a form we can bear. Tragically, my father could have been that North Dakota farmer. My father's basic position on love was: He *married* my mother and *promised* a lifetime commitment. The sacrament and the commitment were sufficient. He needn't *say* more. When you factor in my father's need to keep the lid on his wartime burdens, you may understand that to open the lid just a little bit by verbally expressing his love for my mother risked blowing his lid off completely.

My mother's position on the issue, naturally, was quite different. She wanted my father to be more verbal and more demonstrative of his love for her. She wanted to *hear* him say to her that he loved her. I suppose you might say this was the age-old difference between men and women: men—Mars/women—Venus. In the last few years before her death in 1999, my mother confided in me she had a deep hunger and longing to hear him express his love for her from their marriage's beginning in 1937, until my father's death in 1985. The best she could get from my father, apart from his working, paying the bills, and his daily devotion, was the lame response from him, "Yeah. Me, too," or, on good days, "Yeah. I love you, too," when my mother would say to him, "I love you."

Over the years, my mother developed a whiny, sing-song way of saying, "I love you." It was not a statement given without conditions. Its tonal quality did not decline at its end. It was a half-supplication and half-demand for a return expression of love. Tonally, it ended with an open-ended question that could not be ignored. Just to get her off your back, you relented, and said, "I love you, too." Neither party was satisfied. My mother had to beg. My father, and for that matter, I, replied in kind, but felt extorted by my mother's neediness. In the process, the prize transmuted from what might have been a golden nugget, freely given, to a chintzy Cracker-Jack toy, reluctantly and painfully yielded up.

My father's reticence was not restricted to my mother. Towards the end of my father's life, I telephoned my father with tears in my eyes. I said, "Dad, I have been thinking and crying. There is a question to which I don't know the answer."

He asked, "What is that?"

I said, "Do you love me? You have never told me that you loved me. Do you?"

My mother, who, by now had got on the other telephone extension, piped up, "Mark, of course *we* love you."

Ever struggling with my mother, I commanded, "Mom, I didn't ask *you*. I need to hear if *Dad* loves me!" By this time, I was sobbing, "Do you love me, Dad?"

He replied, "Yes... I love you, Mark." But, immediately, danger surfaced for my father. That old lid might come off. So he asked me one of his standby questions. "How's your golf game these days?"

My two older brothers loved playing golf, a game my father dearly loved. I hated golf and had given it up years before, when I was a teenager. This fact had slipped my father's mind at what might have been a poignant and redemptive moment for our relationship. "Dad, I am the son who doesn't like to golf."

My father died of a massive heart attack a month later. I was thirty-four years old.

All my life, I have suffered a deep ache in my heart. The poet Robert Bly talks about my generation's *father hunger*. Family friend Steve easily detected this deep, unmet need—this raw, ravenous, and emotional hunger. Steve had a well-tuned sense of what each of his boy victims needed. I needed a father figure and a father's love. What role do you suppose Steve feigned?

The nineteenth century Russian author Leo Tolstoy wrote in *Anna Karenina*, "Happy families are all alike; every unhappy family is unhappy in its own way." Unhappy families adjust. Children adjust. We somehow get our needs met, but not in the way we had hoped. I think my mother found solace and pride in the accomplishments of us children. But, again there was her desperate neediness. My mother felt validated by our successes in everything we did. However, my mother had a certain lack of boundaries. *Our* successes became *her* successes. To a degree, this is true for any proud parent. But, because of *her* lack of boundaries, and *her* need for self-validation in our successes, it seemed she needed to walk away with *our* awards and trophies, as if they were *her* own.

As a teenager, I grew increasingly annoyed with my mother's need. In defense, and as part of a covert rebellion, I wouldn't tell my mother about some achievement or award I was scheduled to get at school. She learned of the award after the fact from a catty mother of one of my classmates. My mother was mortified by this person's remark, "Oh! You mean you didn't know Mark was going to get that award last Tuesday? How is that possible?"

In a very real way, I remained stuck in the rebellious teenager mode for many decades. When my wife and I got married, we planned our non-traditional wedding without consulting my mother. She had her heavy hand in the wedding plans of my two older brothers and my sister before me. I knew my mother would have wheedled her way in and tried to run the entire show in order to meet *her* need for approval. When all the planning was in place, and fairly close to the appointed day, I informed my mother of the date and time of the wedding, and invited her and my father to attend. We had a lovely wedding.

Another example occurred a few years before my mother's death at age eighty. She and I were attending the funeral of my mother's brother-in-law. We were both working our way through a receiving line of the decedent's surviving siblings. A sister of the deceased shook my mother's hand and thanked her for coming to the funeral. As I offered my handshake to this woman, my mother said to her, "This is my son Mark."

The woman, who had known my mother for years, and had, no doubt, heard my mother's gloating over her children many times, asked in a mildly snarky way, "Oh. Is this the highly skilled airline pilot, the award-winning salesman, or the successful attorney?"

Another time toward the end of my mother's life, most of my adult cousins from my mother's side of the family gathered for a family reunion at a downtown hotel. My mother was the only one present from her generation. She asked that her children and each of her nieces and nephews stand up, introduce themselves, and say what line of work they were in. Everybody complied. But I inferred the purpose of my mother's request. I knew where this was going. Still acting in a teenaged rebellious mode, though I was in my forties at the time, I was not going to flatter her. She wanted to shine in her children's comparative glory. Since most of my cousins attending this banquet held labor or blue collar jobs, I decided not to play my mother's game. I was one of the last of my generation to speak that evening. When my turn came, I stood up and told my assembled cousins and their spouses, and my mother, "My name is Mark Douglass. I am a failed attorney." I then sat down to everyone's laughter.

They appreciated my attempt at self-deprecation. Several of my male cousins were present at that dinner. During their teenaged years, they shared the use of that wide lapel, padded shoulder, brown suit. They understood my struggles with my mother. Compared to my family, my cousins' family was less well off. They appreciated my mother showing up with shopping bags full of hand-me-downs for them to wear, but one galling image stayed with them throughout the years. My mother routinely arrived at their home with this welcome charity, wearing her one obvious mark of status, an old, but well cared for mink coat.

They say a boy's primary need and duty is to break away from his mother. No matter how much I sought to achieve this, my mother resisted my need and duty. She never wanted to cut the apron strings. My attempts to break away must have been seen by her, at some level, as another man she loved who did not love her in the way she wanted to be loved and admired. Without her children, and their successes reflecting upon her, who or what would she be? My struggle with my mother began when I was twelve or thirteen years old. It continued for several decades, way beyond my teenaged years. Just a few years before she died on her eightieth birthday, I had finally made peace with her. By then, I no longer felt compelled to childishly and reflexively oppose her. I no longer sought to change her. I just accepted her and loved her for the many good qualities she possessed.

While I was a teenager, however, Steve saw this natural struggle as an opportunity. He fanned the flames of my rebellion against my mother when talking with me. When talking with my mother, he acted as if he was the town fire chief doing everything he could possibly do to put out the conflagration.

Did I ever stand a chance against such forces? If I struggled to free myself from the relatively benign presence of my mother, what level of struggle would ultimately be necessary to free myself from the devil, incarnate, our family friend Steve? The trick would be whether I would escape his snare with my life and soul intact. Or whether I would die in the process.

CHAPTER FOUR

Realizing Who's Dangerous

I have endured deep and genuine sadness over my childhood molestation. I have worked through a great deal of this sadness. Two areas of sadness persist. First, whenever I see a twelve-year-old boy, I think *My God! Was I that young when Steve began molesting me?* I also have such a longing for the twelve-year-old boy within me who was never allowed to grow to maturity in a normal fashion. Secondly, I feel sadness for children and teenagers today who live confined lives, over-protected by their parents because of a general hysteria about *stranger danger*.

In contrast to today's relative imprisonment of children and teenagers, my parents gave us children, an incredible amount of freedom. My grade school was about a mile from our home. Each day, I walked to school, back home for lunch, back to school, and at the end of the day, back home again. When you include the running around we children did during twice-a-day recess, and playing after school each day, I routinely walked at least five miles a day.

When I was old enough to ride a bicycle, on weekends and during vacations from school, I rode and rode, all day long, with my neighborhood friends. On occasion, about when I was ten years old, I took some bicycle trips quite far afield from home. One time, a friend and I rode several miles from our home, exploring the world. My friend began to cry, fearing we were lost. I did not, because I knew I would find a way home, or we would get home by doubling back the way we had come. Another time, the summer between fourth and fifth grades, several boys and I rode our bicycles from our quiet neighborhood about five miles to downtown Minneapolis, with all its traffic. There, we spent our pocket change at a penny arcade and at a movie matinée of *The 13 Ghosts*.

During the winter, we would go out in the snow and play for hours on end, building snowmen, or going off to the park near our grade school to slide or toboggan. Sometimes, in mid-winter, on a day when we children had become terribly stir-crazy from watching too much television, my mother would order us outside of the house, telling us not to return until dinnertime.

My parents were quite *laissez-faire* about where we were during non-school days. They were probably less restrictive than many of my friends' parents. My parents were rather trusting about the world. They knew if we got into difficulty, we would call home, or we would solve the problem ourselves. I think this attitude helped us children become self-reliant adults.

Of course, it was a different age. It seems as if we enjoyed a safer society back in the 1950s even though predators such as Steve lived among us. Certainly, there were risks in our childhood, but there was one large force that worked in favor of our safety. The greatest factor in our personal safety was that there were mothers everywhere. If you, as a child, misbehaved, one of *those* mothers would call *your* mother. There would be hell to pay when you got home. These mothers and other adults felt no aversion to making judgments about your behavior, and enforcing those judgments. Today, far fewer mothers remain at home. Also, adults, in general, are loathe to discipline errant children for fear of being labeled judgmental or being sued.

Then, we children got plenty of exercise. Today, children seldom walk to school. Poisoned by television, today's parents fear their children will be grabbed off the street and will never be heard from again. They fear this even though such occurrences are, statistically, about as likely as being struck by lightning. Today, children don't go down to the park in hopes of finding other friends for a pick-up game of what used to be called sandlot baseball. In our old neighborhood, these baseball teams would include children as young as seven or eight and as old as fifteen. For the younger children, often the rules of the game were tailored to accommodate their skills. We negotiated. There was a continual give-and-take.

Children today get some exercise, but their lives are so scheduled and regimented. Little children don't go to the park or the playground with their friends. Instead, their parents set up play-dates at another child's home. Sandlot baseball is scheduled and segregated into age groups and highly structured as Little League. When I was a child, I was only allowed a few hours of television a day before my mother would kick me out of the house to get some exercise interacting with other children. Today, children sit in front of their televisions, their computers, or their video games while snacking on chips and nursing a soft drink. Is it any wonder the media and health professionals bemoan our children's obesity problem?

Most importantly, every aspect of our lives in the 1950s was *not* saturated by media and its scaremongering. Today it is. Today, we are a nation that is both whipped up into a frenzy and paralyzed by fear. We parents fear so much for the well-being of our children, we *deprive* them of their childhoods. We pick them up and drop them off, even though every hour in a car exposes the children to an incredible risk of injury from car accidents. To keep track of them, we give young children cell phones. Some parents place GPS devices on their children or in their children's backpacks. Don't you suppose a kidnapper would ditch the cell phone and the GPS device at his first opportunity?

A couple years ago, I witnessed an incredible public display of this fear. A Level III sexual offender finished his jail sentence and had been paroled. Under Minnesota law, he registered his new address with the parole authorities. The authorities, in turn, notified everybody within a certain distance of the convicted felon's new address. A public hearing was held at a nearby elementary school. The meeting was highly emotional and its atmosphere was that of a lynch mob. Had someone handed out pitch forks, hoes, and shovels, the group, dressed in appropriate period clothing, could have auditioned for the crowd scenes of a Frankenstein movie. People were desperately wondering how their children could possibly be safe with such a monster nearby. Some people wondered, and asked, just how close to tar-and-feathering could they go without violating the law themselves. I sat in this packed school gymnasium and was amazed. Even though I had been repeatedly molested as a child by Steve, I actually felt sorry for the paroled felon.

Dr. Carla van Dam, in her book, *The Socially Skilled Child Molester*, suggests groups of concerned parents such as this one often fail to understand their children may face greater risks from convicted sexual offenders classified as Level I or Level II, as well as from *unidentified* child molesters in society, at large. The more socially skilled sexual offenders often escape detection or are not treated harshly by the criminal justice system.

It was quite possible even in the midst of the crowd in that school gymnasium there were undetected sexual offenders more dangerous than the danger posed by that one, *known*, recently paroled, child molester.

In a more mundane example of parental fear, but in a similar vein, I was in a grocery store checkout line a couple years ago. Behind me were a mother and a young child. I spoke to the child briefly about a book he was reading, a book my own children had loved when they were younger. The child looked up at his mother in fear, yet with a look of seeking permission. He didn't have to speak. The mother answered his question. The mother said, "Yes, you may talk with this man." She then proudly proclaimed to me in a self-congratulatory and beaming manner, "We have taught our children to never talk to strangers."

I could not banish from my mind how idiotic this woman seemed to me. I thought to myself, *Just who should the child seek help from if he were lost on a downtown commercial street or in a busy suburban shopping mall? Aren't sales clerks and security guards strangers? What about police officers? Aren't they strangers, too?*

Dr. Carla van Dam divides the world of child molesters into two basic groups: grabbers and groomers. Grabbers are the cartoon-like stereotype of a child molester held by so many parents today. They are the kind about which the parents at the sexual offender neighborhood meeting near my home were getting so worked up. Grabbers are the subject of so many television crime dramas that play upon our deeply held fears about our children's safety. The stranger danger that we indoctrinate into our children is done with this type of child molester in mind. Grabbers definitely exist. They *are* very dangerous. Yet, they are, in reality, only a small portion of the child molesting population that lives among us.

The second group Dr. van Dam discusses is a much larger group, which she calls groomers. These child molesters live next door or down the street. They teach our children in our schools. They coach our children's athletic teams. They care for our children at day-care centers. They take communion with us at church. They may even administer communion. They are our friends and relatives. They are respected men, primarily, but sometimes, women, of the community.

Steve, our close family friend, was not a grabber—at least when I knew him. He was a groomer. Since my grandmother was his day-care provider from the time of his birth in 1927 until he entered kindergarten in 1933, my mother and her sisters looked upon him almost as though he was their little brother. Hence, when he grew to manhood, although he was an only child, he was well ensconced within our family and my mother's extended family. Steve played on this relationship and abused my parents', my aunts', and my uncles' trust. Although we didn't address him as such, Steve was, essentially, my uncle.

Steve owned a neighborhood business that, like today's franchise restaurants, employed a lot of teenagers throughout the years. With each young man who came into his employ, Steve applied a careful day-to-day screening of his vulnerabilities. With each young man, Steve attempted to fathom the strength and security of his relationship with his family. Steve was particularly focused on boys just on the cusp of puberty—say age twelve or thirteen. Steve certainly did not molest every young man who came to work for him, but from his employees he would groom each teenaged child. Where he found weakness and vulnerability, he would invest more time and effort. Where he found greater parental neglect, Steve sought to become a warm and caring father figure to each vulnerable child and a friend to the child's parents.

Throughout this grooming process, he advanced his boundary violations ever so slowly, such that if the boy or his parents objected or stiffened their resistance, Steve could quickly and strategically retreat from his campaign towards sexual conquest. If either the boy or his parents voiced their objections, Steve would put on an act of high dudgeon, accusing them of being ungrateful and deeply disturbed in their thinking.

Above all, he had an acute sense for what each boy needed or wanted. He then readily gave out attention, gifts, affection, employment, the use of cars, loans of extra spending money, travel, food, alcohol, tobacco—whatever each boy needed or craved.

Steve spent his adult life abusing children. He was occasionally challenged by some of the boys' parents, but Steve was never arrested or charged with criminal sexual conduct or lewd behavior. He never went to jail for this conduct.

My parents were not oblivious to the problem of child molestation. When I was an elementary school child, I recall my mother instructing my little sister, "When you go to the park or the playground to play, if you ever see a man with his pants fly open, be sure to run away as fast as you can." Well, I don't know if my little sister understood the import of our mother's message, but I was left scratching my head unable to understand why any male, young or old, would walk around with his "barn door" open. Heck! The "cow" might get out. Everybody knew that. How embarrassing!

Just like the rabid crowd I witnessed at the neighborhood meeting about the paroled sexual offender, my mother held in her mind a cartoon or a caricature of a flasher or a child molester. Yet, two or three times a week she would happily serve breakfast to our family friend Steve. After all, he was so helpful and so generous. He spent time with us boys, and he gladly drove us kids to our junior and senior high schools. Being a bachelor, he also dined with us as family at Christmas, Thanksgiving, and Easter. Throughout the rest of the year he sated his other appetite—also in our home.

CHAPTER

FIVE

A Pre-teen Boy's Troubles

When, in the early 1980s, I first went public with the facts of my abuse, I was, emotionally and psychologically, really quite numb. Nevertheless, I went public in a big way. Against my therapist's advice, I decided my case would be a newsworthy case, because the issue of male sexual abuse was just emerging in the media. At the time, the local media was having a heyday about a child abuse ring uncovered in a suburban metropolitan county. The news was so strange and so horrid, people wanted to discount it. The prevailing view was sexual child abuse was restricted to the poor and the lower class, occurring only in isolated farms and trailer parks.

In contrast, I grew up in a neighborhood peppered largely with mansions, but in-filled with a variety of different sized and styled houses. When the larger houses were originally built between 1900 and 1920, the neighborhood was quite in demand. Today, this neighborhood is in extremely high demand. However, during the 1950s and 1960s, many of these homes needed repair and redecoration. For most home buyers, the suburbs held more attraction. The two homes in which our family lived during my childhood were fixer-uppers or handyman's specials. Through my parents' ongoing efforts, our homes became quite lovely and valuable. With the aid of my parents' sweat equity, and with inflation, my parents eventually sold both properties at a profit.

Although my father was a dentist, we were not as well off as many of my schoolmates' families. My friends' fathers were doctors, psychologists, lawyers, professors, and executives. Many of them belonged to country clubs, an extravagance my parents felt was simply out of the question. We children all attended our local public grade school. At the beginning of junior high school, however, there was a great divide. Several of the girls in my sixth grade class left the public schools to attend the private girls' school, Northrup Collegiate Girls' School. Most of the bright, striving boys I knew in my sixth grade class, went on to expensive private boys' schools in Minneapolis such as Breck, Blake, or University High School.

I remember desperately wanting to accompany my friends to these tony schools. I pleaded with my parents to pay my way at one of them. My father simply and clearly informed me he just could not afford the tuition. In addition, he felt families that sent their children to such schools were social climbing. At the time, I felt life had dealt me a cruel blow. Yet life turned, what first appeared to me as a loss, into a great boon. With the exodus of so many of my intelligent, athletic, striving grade school classmates to local private schools, I was thrust into positions of leadership in my public junior high and high school. These positions, coupled with my grades, made me an attractive candidate for elite colleges. In my senior year, when I applied to Harvard University, the three leading candidates from Minneapolis were me, and two of my best friends from grade school who had gone on to private school in hopes of bettering their chances of getting into an elite college. I, the public school student, was given the nod.

For those of my college bound grade school classmates who did not go on to private schools, my junior high school and my high school had special programs set up to cater to us. We were expected to go on to college by our families and into the same kind of high paying and high status jobs our parents held.

For college, I attended and graduated from Harvard University in Cambridge, Massachusetts. I returned to Minnesota to go to law school at Hamline University School of Law in St. Paul. I was now a lawyer. What better man-bites-dog media story could there be than mine? *EXTRA! EXTRA! Even rich boys get diddled!*

In the early 1980s, a reporter with one of our major metropolitan television stations interviewed me for a television news special about child sexual abuse, a just emerging news topic. While we were filming the interview, it was clear to me the reporter hoped I might be able to express more emotion while on camera. I just couldn't do it. I had all the right words down pat, but my affect was controlled and numb. Naturally, like my father, I had *my* lid on tight.

Over the years, my emotions did bubble to the surface. Sometimes, they erupted with great force and drama. There was a time when I raged against Steve. There was a time when I raged against my parents. Since my rage against my parents emerged, largely, after my father's death in 1985, my mother bore the brunt it. I thought and wondered how could they have not seen what was going on with Steve? In contrast to my outward rage, there was a great deal of inner rage and sadness, which, every few years, threw me into the depths of a major depression. I am currently in my mid-fifties. I feel I am finally getting a measured perspective on the events of my childhood. I have finally become optimistic about life and my future.

We childhood victims of sexual abuse often journey along a long and lonely path of recovery. Over time and with the help of others, we become survivors of sexual abuse. If we continue on our path, and continue to heal and grow, the issue of sexual abuse does not burn so hotly within us. Certainly, our sexual abuse history is a part of us, but it does not have to define us, to the exclusion of all the other things we do and enjoy in this life.

I know I went from a silence of seventeen years, to wanting to stand up and shout from the rooftops the horrid details of my teenaged years. I went from silence to wanting to speak the unspeakable, whether or not anybody else wanted to hear about it. Thank God, I have been blessed by an understanding wife this past quarter century. During most of this time, I have spoken about my abuse, processed my abuse, spoken some more from a slightly different viewpoint, further processed my abuse, and then spoken yet some more. My wife has lovingly and patiently listened to me. I have been incredibly blessed by her presence and her partnership.

Currently, I am at a stage where having spoken the unspeakable, I have come to accept the unacceptable about what happened to me at Steve's hands. I am usually at peace with this, but short bursts of anger still do emerge from time to time. These slight, private, eruptions pose no danger to me or those about me. They do, however, remind me I still have some inner work to do in order to heal fully.

I look forward to what to me looks like a final stage for me. I hope, soon, to be able to forgive the unforgivable. I have not quite arrived at this stage, but I see the lights of this promised land on the horizon.

As I gain this new perspective, I realize the society and the family environment in which I grew up were complicated. More and more, I realize there were many factors that groomed me and set me up for the abuse by Steve. In the 1950s, we lived in relative isolation from so many problems of the world. We got much of our information from the newspapers, a moderate and somewhat intellectual source. Although we had television, its news coverage was restrained by today's standards. Today, we are exposed to so much media, it is dizzying. In an effort to achieve high ratings and market share, the media airs the most heart wrenching, emotional, and often, bizarre stories possible. The media today screams in our face about so many conditions—societal, family, and personal. The cry is that the government should do something about these problems. In the 1950s, the same conditions existed, but we often turned away in the belief that certain things are better dealt with in private, within the family.

In my family, there was, of course, my father's desire for privacy. There was his need for emotional and psychological stability and for insuring that his own tranquility was not disturbed by the trying demands of raising four children. There was my mother's loneliness. There was her unquenchable neediness— her need for constant love and approval. Despite this, most observers would have said my parents were fine people. Even with their faults, as a parent, I can *now* see and empathize with them. They were good, hard working, responsible people, but they were also flawed people. They had a good life despite their flaws. If they could have addressed some of their human failings, their lives together might have been fuller and more satisfying.

Most importantly, if they had addressed their personal flaws, they might not have shifted the burden of parenting *our parents* to us children. I think we children became their psychological parents. Our family roles were reversed. We children took care of their emotional and psychological needs. For me, at least, I think this groomed me for later taking care of Steve's needs. In an odd sort of way, in the course of becoming his victim, I became his caretaker. My parents' flaws inadvertently sacrificed a part of my childhood. Steve's flaws purposely decimated my teenaged and young adulthood years.

Because of Steve, my childhood ended when I was twelve years old. The concept of the *inner child* bandied about in psychological and pseudo-psychological discussions always seemed to me corny and a bit overdone. Yet, because of Steve's conduct, my *inner child* was placed in a prison at age twelve. Securely locked away, that child could only be released through much effort, struggle, and therapy over the years.

Another aspect of my upbringing affected my suitability for Steve's molestation of me. This arose from my relationship with my brothers, coupled with my parents' failure to intervene on my behalf. My eldest brother is eight years older than I am. My other brother is three years older than I am. We have a younger sister, but I want to focus on the relationship among brothers.

I suspect that families having only sons are, generally speaking, rough and tumble environments. Our home was like that. My eldest brother would lord it over my other brother. Together, they would lord it over me. Or, my oldest brother would physically dominate my other brother. This brother would then dominate me. An example of this was a game my brothers called the Jefferson-99, a game they learned from their classmates at Jefferson Junior High School. In this game, the older, larger brother would wrestle the younger, smaller brother to the floor and onto his back. The older brother would sit on the younger brother's chest and arms, pinning him to the floor. Then the older brother would take the knuckle of his middle finger and repeatedly rap upon the pinned brother's forehead. He would rap and count with each rap up to the requisite ninety-nine. The rapping was not so hard as to leave a bruise, but it, nevertheless, hurt the weaker, younger child. It was termed a *game*, but it was a mild form of *torture*. Certainly, its aim was to overpower and to humiliate.

Power, dominance, and humiliation were the critical elements. Likewise, a verbal banter went back and forth between my older brothers that sounded like a Don Rickles' nightclub act. I suppose this sparring was okay between them. In fact, my two older brothers have always been quite close and remain so, even today. They still engage in this verbal one-upmanship, which degrades into greater and greater insults to the person and the manhood of the other.

Well, I was the youngest brother. I was, for some reason, more sensitive. My brothers really didn't care about my sensitivity. They played these games against me, exerting their power and dominance over me until I would break down in tears of frustration, rage, and humiliation.

In another example, in comparison to my older brothers, I was not as athletically coordinated as they were. A five-year-old could not hit a baseball with the same effectiveness or skill as an eight-year-old or a thirteen-year-old, even if I wanted to. My attempts to measure up to my brothers' abilities were met with a tirade of taunts about my being uncoordinated and lacking in athletic talent. Hopelessly uncoordinated! A sissy! A girl!

When I was learning to ice skate, rather than face these taunts, each winter evening after dinner, I would go down to the local ice rink in the dark, lace up my skates, and fail *or* succeed in private, until I mastered the skill. I think because of this atmosphere of ridicule, I never became interested in high school team sports. However, I think, unconsciously, I tried to show my brothers up when I went to Harvard. It wasn't in football or baseball, or ice skating for that matter, but I, nevertheless, became an Ivy League athlete. I earned two varsity letters and became the captain of the Harvard University rifle team.

In the face of this ongoing ridicule by my brothers, my parents seldom stepped in. Now I recognize there are good arguments for letting children work things out themselves. In fact, if a parent intervenes too much, the well intentioned intervention can actually foster more problems among the children. What I do know is that when I played with my own male friends and attempted the Jefferson-99 game upon them, they screamed in terror. Their mothers quickly came to their rescue and either lectured me, or they ordered me out of their homes. In bewilderment, I returned home. What had I done wrong? I was only playing the *games* my brothers taught me.

A more telling example of my parents' failure to protect arose at our summer lake cabin in northern Minnesota. My father had a lifelong friend named Andy, who grew up down the road from my father's home during their childhood. Andy, his wife, and family often socialized with our family. When Andy and his family moved away to another state, Andy and his family returned to Minnesota every Fourth of July, year after year, to vacation with our family at our lake cabin. We spent ten days playing, fishing, waterskiing, and golfing.

Andy told wonderfully funny stories, anecdotes, and jokes. But he also turned his humor upon those around him. To his children, and to us children, he started joking and riding us about something. He wouldn't let up. We had to learn to joke back or we had to bear it. Well, children are not usually as quick witted as adults. Again, maybe I was just too sensitive, but Andy's aim eventually got around to me. Sometimes, his taunts ended in my tears. On one occasion, it happened when Andy joined us children, while we were swimming at the beach in front of our family cabin.

For ten days each summer, we shared a two-room cabin that had no modern conveniences. The adults needed to bathe every few days. One day, Andy needed to bathe. He came down to the lake where we children were cavorting in the water, oblivious to its chill. With a washcloth and a bar of soap in hand, he slowly worked his way into the cold lake water. The other children joked with him about his dislike of the cold water. Hadn't he ever been swimming in a lake before? He tried to joke back, but was preoccupied with the frigid water temperature. As the egging-on rose in tempo, I jokingly threatened to splash him. After all, he always joked with us. Couldn't we joke in our own way? My brothers and Andy's children dared me to splash him. Andy warned me not to splash him. Because of Andy's incessant jesting over the years, I did not take his warning seriously. I just thought it was part of the usual give-and-take. I thought if he could dish it out, then he could also take it. The difference here was that, for once, I had gained the upper hand in the teasing. Or so I thought. I splashed him. Andy erupted with incredible anger. He lunged at me and slapped me hard across the face, yelling at me, "Didn't I tell you not to splash me?"

I was merely eleven or twelve years old at the time—not quite a boy and not yet a man. Comparatively speaking, I was still powerless to deal with the situation at hand and with the ways of adults. Andy's slap stung my face *and* my pride. I was completely appalled. I was drenched from swimming, but also drenched with humiliation and shame. Why couldn't Andy take a joke? He was the one who was always joking around. I burst into hot, angry tears, left the water, and went up to the cabin.

When I got up to the cabin, still in tears, I complained with incredulity to my father, "Andy hit me!"

My father asked me, "Well, what did you do to provoke him?"

Given the choice between my father's friend and me, my father made no effort to back me up or inquire into the matter with Andy. Most importantly, my father made no effort to broker a rapprochement between me and Andy. My father could have talked with Andy. Together, they could have come to me to discuss the matter. Andy could have tried to explain to me just how cold the lake water was to an adult his age. He could have explained the shock of the splashed water was just that, a shock. He could have explained that he just flew off the handle. Andy might have even apologized to me. But, no. I was left to my shame, humiliation, and my anger. I was left to conclude that my father would side with his adult friend and not with me, his son. I concluded, my father wouldn't jeopardize his friendship in order to protect me. Steve, of course, was one of my father's other close friends.

Because, I came into Steve's clutches soon thereafter, I never again vacationed at our northern Minnesota cabin when Andy and his family came up to our cabin for each successive Fourth of July. A little more than a decade later, I was in the receiving line at my sister's wedding. I was no longer a thin, scrawny eleven-year-old. I was in my mid-twenties and was overweight. Andy and his wife attended the wedding. When he came up to shake my hand, he asked, "So. How are you, *FATSO*?"

Because, I was now an adult, and could fairly deal with him on his own terms, I shook his hand, glared at him, and forcefully replied, "Just fine. *YOU OLD FART!*" He was non-plussed and shocked that I actually stood up to his bullying attempts at humor. He quickly retreated to the safety of conversing with next person in the receiving line. I never spoke to him again.

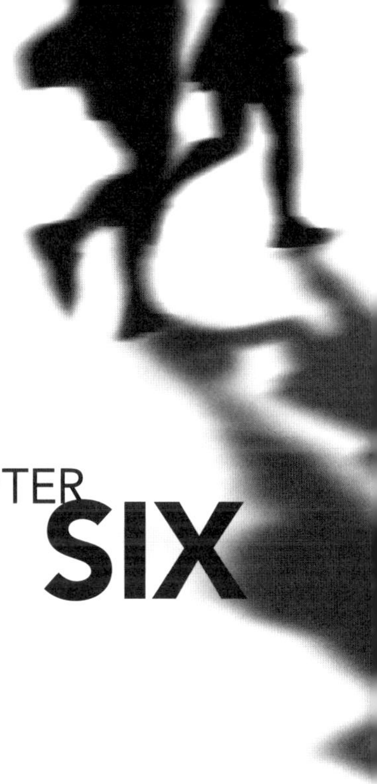

CHAPTER SIX

The Serpent Appears

Steve was more than a close family friend. Steve was, for all practical purposes, my uncle. His sexual abuse of me was, psychologically speaking, incest—not merely sexual abuse.

Steve was born in Minneapolis in 1927. His mother was a respected English teacher at the working class neighborhood high school near my mother's family home. His father had been a business executive, but was convicted of embezzlement and sentenced to several years imprisonment. As a result, Steve's mother and father divorced when Steve was an infant. The divorce decree awarded custody to Steve's mother. Steve's mother was single again after her divorce, but she wasn't alone. She had a child to take care of. She needed to teach in order to make ends meet. She needed somebody to take care of her child during the school day in order to continue working. My mother's family lived only a few blocks from the high school where Steve's mother taught.

My grandmother did many things to bring extra income into the family coffers. She did extra laundry. She baked bread and pies for a nearby bakery. When Steve's mother needed what we now call day-care services, my grandmother readily agreed to provide them. My grandmother was Steve's other mother from shortly after he was born until he started attending school full-time in the first grade. Thus, for about seven years, my grandmother baby-sat Steve. For her, this was a chance to earn some more money for her family of five daughters. It was also her chance to raise a son. As a result of my grandmother's generosity and giving heart, Steve became my mother's and her sisters' little brother. In the years to come, Steve played upon this relationship as the baby brother in order to gain the trust of his sisters, *and* their boys.

When I first met Steve, he lived with his mother in a mansion that was only about a mile and a half away from our home. It was a beautiful building built at great expense just before World War I, but by the 1950s was in need of repair. This mansion had really lovely woodwork and trim. The living room had built-in bookshelves and a very substantial mantel above the fireplace, one of several in the home. Atop this mantel, Steve placed a cut glass candy dish filled to the brim with M&Ms. At least, he kept it full when I began to visiting his home several afternoons a week on my way home from my junior high school.

Looking back over the years, I am certain the bountifully filled cut glass candy dish was set atop the mantel just for me. You see, my grandfather was a dentist and my father was a dentist. In our home, candy was not an option—or at least, it was seldom an option. The fact that we came from such a dental heritage was one factor. Another factor was there were four of us children. My mother ran the household on a strict monthly budget. Trying to supply candy and soft drinks to us children would have significantly cut into the monthly food budget. That is not to say we were totally deprived of sweets. My mother had a sweet tooth and she loved to bake. Thus, for our family, she would make pies, cakes, cookies, and delights such as caramel rolls. But these were usually reserved for dessert after our supper or for holidays. My father had a sweet tooth, too. He kept a box of Hershey bars along with a few cartons of Lucky Strike cigarettes stashed up high in his bedroom closet. But these candy bars were strictly off limits. At Halloween, we were allowed to collect as large a treasure trove of candy as we were able, and could budget its consumption over the days and weeks afterwards. Also there were no restrictions on our using the money we made on our paper routes. If we wanted to spend it on candy, it was our money to spend. But the monthly household budget money was not to be spent on candy or soft drinks.

At our home we seldom had soft drinks. I remember often playing at my friend Tom's house afternoons after school. There, I was completely astounded that his parents bought several cases of bottled soft drinks each month. As Tom's guests, we were free to drink as many bottles as we wanted to. This was highly unusual in the 1950s and 1960s generally, and unheard of in my home.

Also at Tom's house, his mother set out cake, brownies, or Rice Krispy bars for Tom and his after-school guests. When playing at Tom's house, I asked, "Do you really mean we can have some? Are you sure it is not dessert for after your dinner, tonight?" Despite Tom's assurances, as I indulged, I could almost hear my mother yelling, "Put that down! You know we are saving that for dessert tonight!"

Of course, Steve with his highly tuned pedophilic antennae, discovered I had a sweet tooth not satisfied at home. What a simple investment for him to buy a few extra bags of M&Ms when he did his grocery shopping. Those M&Ms played a small, but calculated, part of his overall plan of seducing me the summer of 1963.

Not only did Steve indulge my sweet tooth. He also further separated me from my family by the simple act of taking me to a restaurant. My father's income from dentistry fluctuated from month to month throughout the year. Such fluctuations are the bane of self-employment. Because life can be feast or famine, the self-employed person often feels as if there is never enough money on hand. Also, since both my parents lived through the Great Depression, both felt it important to keep the family's spending within a budget, and whenever possible, to save for a rainy day. One of the things that can kill a family budget, then as well as now, is the expense of restaurant dining—particularly when you must feed six mouths—two adults and four growing kids. Back in the 1950s and 1960s, there were far fewer fast food restaurants than today. Meals at our home were seldom varied by fast food, except for the rare moment when my father would bring home take-out food from a downtown Chinese restaurant. The other exception to home cooked meals occurred on some Friday afternoons during the summer. When we drove up to our northern Minnesota lake cabin for the weekend, we would dine at Paul's Restaurant in Milaca, which was roughly the half way point between our home and our cabin. As a family, we probably dined out fewer than fifteen times during the year.

Knowing this, Steve often took my brother and me to a restaurant that served pancakes and waffles. There we were treated to waffles smothered in fruit compote, whipped cream, and maple syrup. We even ordered hot chocolate if we wanted. When it came time to pay the bill, there were no discussions about how expensive it was, or how this outing affected the week's food budget. The waitress presented the bill. Steve handed me or my brother the money. We went to the cashier to pay, and we were even allowed to buy a mint patty or a candy bar for each of us. As kids, we thought this incredibly generous of Steve. It was also a bit sinful, in a way, because of our family's concern about too many sweets, sensible nutrition, and money. Sweets and candy were the forbidden fruit. Steve was the serpent.

Of course, somewhere in the course of such an outing, Steve opined something to the effect of, "You know, I just can't quite understand why your parents don't take you to restaurants more often than they do." Neither my brother nor I were sophisticated enough to realize we were being manipulated just as the serpent manipulated Adam and Eve in the Garden of Eden. Steve carefully and stealthily sowed seeds of doubt and discontent in our teenaged minds and hearts. Steve stated and planted the idea, "If your parents loved you, they would take care of you the way I do." I was tempted to believe him.

CHAPTER SEVEN

Divide and Conquer

From the time of my first haircut until age twelve, my mother was our family barber. She had a cardboard box in which she stored an electric hair clipper, a barber's shears, a couple combs, a hairbrush, an old bed sheet, and a couple large safety pins. About once every two weeks, she placed a chair in the middle of the basement floor, took the cardboard box down from the shelf, and set out the haircutting tools. Mother's barbershop was open. My father and each of us children submitted to her shears. I really don't know if she kept a schedule as to when her barbershop opened. It was usually on the weekend. More importantly, it opened when my mother looked at one of us and decided our locks had become too decadent. In the 1950s era of crew cuts, this standard was fairly easily measured, although it was her standard, not ours.

Of course, the ever present thought of money was an issue. Why would anyone send their children to a real barbershop if a passable job could be done at home? Cutting our hair was a way in which our mother assured we looked presentable to the world at a budget saving price.

I think she deeply felt, or perhaps feared, that our neighbors, our teachers, and others looked upon how well or ill-kept we appeared, and ascribed our appearance to her skills as a mother. (On this particular issue, as an adult, I almost never leave home without shaving. I seldom wear ratty clothes unless I am doing yard work or I am taking a short trip to the hardware store. When traveling by air, I almost always wear a coat and tie. And finally, I almost never wear a T-shirt or a sweatshirt with any sort of message emblazoned on its front or back.)

As a child, I didn't understand there was a more important aspect to having one's hair cut by our mother. I don't really know if my mother consciously thought about it, either. The time each of us children sat in mother's barber chair was a time in which she was talking with us, spending time with us, and touching us in a healthy and caring manner. It was a time we talked and a time in which she listened, provided we kept still while she tried to make sure the haircut was done evenly and somewhat aesthetically. Such a connection between parent and child was something Steve could not allow to continue if he was to successfully and subtly cut us adrift from our family's love and support.

Two forces of the world helped Steve's evil plan. First, each of us boys encountered puberty and the spirit of rebelliousness that accompanied it. The second was the influence of the Beatles and all the other rock stars. Crew cuts were out. Long hair was in. My mother just had to close up shop, except to give my father a regular trim.

Of course, Steve incited and fed our rebellion. He took my brother and me to a real men's barbershop. He, and he alone, introduced us to a traditional aspect of a man's world, but *he* was always present and *he* paid the barber. *He* controlled the entire process, even giving instructions to the barber. Insidiously, he also was certain to comment, "Well, now! That's a *real* haircut! It looks so much better than any of your mother's haircuts!"

Steve watched and observed our family to determine other inroads he could make with us.

Beginning when I was about seven years old, I often took the bus downtown to my father's dental office. The Number One bus ran along a residential street that was a block away from our home. It ran downtown along a busy commercial street that paralleled the street my father's office building was on. I paid my bus fare of fifteen cents, sat directly across the aisle from the driver. The driver made sure I got off at Seventh Street and Hennepin Avenue. I walked directly to my father's office at Seventh Street and Marquette Avenue, two blocks away. When I reached it, I took the elevators up to the eighth floor, walked down the corridor, and entered my father's office.

Today, most people would find this to be completely outrageous. But back in the 1950s and the 1960s, there was not the "homeless problem" we have today. Rightly or wrongly, in the 1950s, most mentally ill people, alcoholic, or drug addicted people who could not keep and maintain a job were kept off the streets and housed in asylums or jails. Therefore, it was not as dangerous to send a child of a certain age on the public transit downtown as it might be today.

As I got to be nine or ten years old, I was allowed to go downtown by myself to the movies, which were shown in the great movie palaces of the 1920s, still barely remaining in business despite competition from suburban movie houses and from television. I saw movies shown at the Orpheum, Pantages, Lyric, World, Academy, Gopher, and the Academy theaters. The cost for a child my age was thirty-five cents. Thus began my love of movies. When I became a teenager, I also began watching more movies on television, particularly NBC's *Saturday Night at the Movies*. During vacation from school, I would also watch afternoon and sometimes late-night movies on local television.

Naturally, Steve observed that I liked going to the movies. So once a week, or so, he would take me to a first-run movie. As a special treat, he took me to our local Cinerama theater, the Cooper Theater. Cinerama shows were really spectacular, comparable in some ways to today's IMAX theaters. Steve paid for the tickets and I ate candy, a soft drink, and popcorn without worrying about the cost.

The fact that my parents were so permissive in allowing me to travel downtown and to go to movies by myself was not really outrageous for the times, but it signaled to Steve that here was a child who was not under close parental supervision. Here was a child he could become involved with and his parents would not inquire too closely. Besides, he was my "uncle." What was not to trust?

If I liked candy, popcorn, and entertainment, what better place was there to find these than at the Minnesota State Fair? Minnesota, with its large farming sector, has one of the largest state fairs in the nation. My cousins went to the fair every year with their parents, my aunt and uncle. My older brothers went regularly. I remember when I was about five years old, my mother taking my two older brothers to the fair. I was so forlorn that I could not go with them. But my mother was trying to be practical. A day at the state fair was, generally, too much for a five-year-old, unless you brought along a coaster wagon or large stroller to carry him once he became cranky and could go no further. I did receive a consolation prize, a stuffed panda bear, won or purchased by my oldest brother.

When I was about eight or nine, my uncle from Oregon, an engineer, took me to the state fair. We, of course, spent most of the day up on Machinery Hill looking at tractors, plows, and combines. Most of the remainder of the day, we looked at cows, pigs, horses, chickens, and crop exhibits. Towards the end of the day, he finally took me to the Midway where all the rides and carnival games-of-chance were. He allowed me to ride no more than a couple rides. Uncle Ray actually joined me on a ride in the Mad Mouse. The Mad Mouse was a roller coaster in which the individual cars bore a cartoon resemblance to a pointy-nosed mouse. I sat in front. He sat behind me. The ride had numerous sharp, very sharp, turns during which, from my vantage point, I felt the car was going to fall off the track. After that day at the state fair, I did not return until I reached age twelve.

My father never took me to the state fair. Looking back, I suspect he just could not stand the crowds or the spending of money on frivolous things. The dislike of crowds, no doubt, arose from his experiences as a prisoner of war in Nazi Germany. Of course, his issue with spending money was perpetual throughout my childhood.

Steve saw another opportunity here. Steve took me to the state fair. We spent some time looking at farm machinery and livestock. But, at the Midway, I was allowed to go on just about as many rides as I wanted. I also ate the many varieties of junk food treats at the fair. Steve's pockets were deep, money was endless, and he seemed so generous. But his generosity was just a part of his overall plan: spend time with me, spend money on me, isolate me, and tell me endless half-truths and lies about my family and about my parents and their lack of love for me. Steve understood the power of his supposed generosity over me, and over my family. To him, it wasn't generosity. It was just the cost of doing business.

We live in a culture where when one receives a gift, one is implicitly obligated to respond with a gift of comparable value. It is an unstated, but firmly fixed, value in our society. To not return the favor of a gift with a gift of comparable value leaves one in a sort of trade deficit. No doubt, our awareness of this unstated rule is why some couples insist on Dutch treat when on a date. In an effort to balance Christmas giving with this rule, businesses may allow holiday office gift exchanges, but with limits of, say, ten dollars per gift. It is probably also the reason when we receive a charity solicitation in the mail, the charity includes return address labels with our names and addresses printed on them. Place the recipient in debt and maybe he will feel compelled to contribute money.

Whenever my mother and father went out to dinner at a restaurant with Steve, my father and Steve engaged in a ritual battle over who paid the bill. My father was already off balance with respect to Steve because Steve was so generous in his giving to us kids. Steve, of course, intended this imbalance. He then added to the imbalance by paying the restaurant tab. My father protested. An agreement was tentatively reached whereby my father promised to pay for the next outing. The ritual battle continued at the next outing.

This gift giving imbalance came up at family birthday parties and also, in its most extravagant form, at Christmastime. Our family opened gifts on Christmas Eve. Steve was always on hand as the guest of honor. After a terrific dinner prepared and served by my mother, we retired to the living room to open our gifts. During many years, the pile of gifts under the Christmas tree was incredibly bountiful. Almost half of the gifts were from Steve to us kids—toys and games and, for us boys, plastic airplane or car models to be assembled, glued, and painted at a later date. As between Steve and my parents, Steve gave some extravagant gifts to them. One Christmas, Steve gave my father an expensive, single-lens reflex, Pentax 35mm camera. My parents, knowing Steve liked boats and all things nautical, bought Steve a lovely model of a sailboat with sails unfurled and the boat plying the waves. They bought it at a jewelry store. It was made of silver and gold plated metal. My parents really had to stretch to buy Steve this gift.

In retrospect, the competition between my parents and Steve was quite sad. In a sense it was even obscene. My parents acted out of good cultural behavior and real gratitude. Steve deliberately manipulated things to ensure my next older brother's and my silence and to keep my parents from inquiring to closely about us. Christmas after Christmas, and birthday after birthday, Steve showered our family with gifts, while throughout the year he molested my brother and me. Part of the obscenity of it all was that a great many of Steve's gifts were merchandise stolen by Steve, or at Steve's direction, from the central warehouse of a well known nationally franchised hardware company!

CHAPTER EIGHT

Isolation and Interrogation

Steve was a large, overpowering man. He lived in a grand house. All the years I knew him, he drove a big car, a Lincoln Continental sedan. When he first began molesting me in 1963, he owned a white, 1960 Lincoln Continental with electric windows, electric locks, black leather upholstery, air conditioning, and what were known as *suicide doors*. This was quite a car. As a youngster, the electric windows and locks were fascinating to me. And air conditioning! Our *house* didn't have air conditioning. Our family car *certainly* didn't have air conditioning. Oddly, today, the features of this luxury car are pretty much standard on the cars most middle class families drive. But, back then, what a set of wheels. What a car!

I don't recall seeing *suicide doors* on any other car but the 1960 Lincoln Continental. These doors were probably more accurately called coach doors, where the front doors are hinged toward the front side of the car, and the back doors are hinged towards the back of the car. These doors were reminiscent of the doors on a luxury horse drawn coach, where a coachman used both his hands to simultaneously open, or close, both doors. I guess I focus on the nickname only because for so many years of my life beginning at age thirteen and ending in my late forties, I regularly entertained thoughts of suicide. This car was emblematic of Steve's seduction and molestation of me. I cannot see a Lincoln without being reminded of Steve. Several years back, I was shocked to learn, I was not alone in making this association.

In October 1989, an eleven-year-old boy named Jacob Wetterling was kidnapped near St. Joseph, Minnesota. Over the years, law enforcement authorities received over 50,000 leads in the case, but Jacob, or his remains, were never found. One newspaper report I read at the time, generally described the suspected kidnapper as a large man armed with a pistol and driving a large sedan, possibly a Lincoln Continental. Anyone having information about such a person was to call the FBI. When I read that in the newspaper, my jaw just dropped. Steve was a large man who owned and drove Lincoln Continentals. He owned numerous guns, including a pistol. He had worked on a construction project many years before in Cold Spring, a community not far from St. Joseph, Minnesota. He had made veiled, indirect threats about murder to me when I was a teenager. Putting all this together, I called the FBI to suggest the special agents might wish to investigate Steve. When I called, I was told Steve was already on their list of suspects. Either the FBI had Steve on some sort of pedophile list that they cross-referenced with Lincoln Continental owners, or one of Steve's abuse victims called the FBI regarding Steve. I was both shocked and, yet, not surprised at all. It confirmed for me what I already knew. If some other person had called in a tip, there were, perhaps, other victims of Steve's I didn't know about. Something scared me a bit, though. Could Steve really be the perpetrator of this violent crime, a crime that probably included murder? If so, Steve was, indeed, a more dangerous and violent man than I had ever fully imagined.

On several years' reflection, before and after Steve's death, I have thought, *He was a large man. He lived in a large house. He drove a large, expensive car. But, in reality he was a very small man—an impostor of a man—a child posing as an adult. Many things large concealed the tiny and the pitiful.*

Steve died in 1992. But something continued to gnaw away at me. Why does he and his Lincoln Continental continue to live on in my mind? In trying to resolve this question, I thought of my father. When my father, a World War II B-17 pilot, was shot down on his first bombing mission over Nazi occupied Europe, he was brought to the German Luftwaffe's central interrogation center in Frankfurt, Germany, called Dulag Luft. There my father was placed in solitary confinement for several days, cut off from his comrades. From time to time, he was let out of solitary confinement and he was brought to his inquisitors for questioning. My father refused to answer their questions. He was then returned to solitary confinement. Later, he was asked again. He gave no answers. He was again returned to solitary. While he was in his dark, windowless cell, alone, cold, hungry, unbathed, and unshaven, firing squads staged mock executions in the adjacent courtyard. He must have wondered if he would soon be standing in front of his own firing squad. These tactics were used upon all captured Allied flyers. Most did not crack under the strain. But enough did that the Nazis gained a great deal of intelligence information about Allied forces and Allied strategies. Isolation and interrogation. Isolation and interrogation.

Steve used his Lincoln Continental as a mobile isolation and interrogation chamber. At first, Steve enticed me to join him for a short ride in his car. Maybe it was just a half hour drive around the Minneapolis city lakes. Near the end of the drive, he took me to an ice cream shop for a treat. Over time, the rides became longer. He drove me on a series of errands. However, instead of only a half hour or an hour, I was in for a two or three hour drive. These drives became longer and longer. Typically, they ended up being twenty to forty miles away from my home. Further than I wished to walk home. Unknowingly, I became Steve's captive.

During these drives he conversed with me in a friendly way. Often the conversation became manipulative. He asked me who I loved most—my mother or my father. Then, no matter how I answered, he twisted things around to show how stupid I was for loving either. He proclaimed, "Any idiot could plainly see that your parents don't love you at all. Your mother loves your oldest brother. Your father loves your next older brother. They both adore your little sister. But, in fact, your parents felt burdened and oppressed by the very fact you were born. They wanted a daughter."

One time, after a long campaign of spending time with me, giving me gifts, and driving me on many isolation and interrogation drives, he asked me to place a dollar value on *our friendship*. I demurred. He insisted. I told him I could not place a monetary value upon friendship. He insisted that I do so. After much cajoling and manipulation, I gave in. I tried to estimate what a large sum of money would be—say the cost of going to college for four years. Based upon my earning power of less than a dollar per day from my morning newspaper route, I proposed the sum of $20,000, just to get him off my back.

He then verbally tore into me. "How could I be so low as to place a dollar value on our friendship—AFTER ALL I HAVE DONE FOR YOU?" He further added, "I am deeply disappointed in you, Mark!" I felt tremendous shame and guilt, but I started to think I was not interested in taking any more rides with Steve.

My older brother and I had our bedrooms on the third floor of our family home. From my bedroom dormer window, I could see the street in front of our home. In the warmer months of the year, I could hear a car drive up and park in front of our home, if I left the dormer window open. If, from my dormer window, or the living room window on the first floor, I saw Steve drive up in front of the house, I ran down to the basement and hid under the stairwell, in the boiler room, or under our billiard table. Sometimes, I ran out the back door of our home and hid in the garage attic. Sometimes, I ran out the back door and over to a friend's house. I just did not want to spend another afternoon, or most of the day, in Steve's Lincoln Continental driving all over town and out into the countryside.

More than forty years later, I don't fully understand why I just didn't say no to Steve when he came by our home, unannounced. He had an incredible way of manipulating and at the same time, persuading me to accompany him. "It will only be a short trip," or "I want to show you something that you will really find interesting." Statements such as these proved to be lies, of course. From my teenage perspective, it so often just seemed hopeless to resist. Steve had my parents wrapped around his little finger. Despite my resistance, Steve groomed me to go along passively with whatever he planned.

During one period, I resisted Steve on some point. He insisted the problem lay with *me*. *I* supposedly had a bad attitude. *I* needed to be straightened out.

He drove me and my brother out into the countryside a distance of about twenty miles from my home to Lake Minnetonka. He told me I had better change *my* attitude and cooperate, or I should just get out and walk. Since I knew where we were, I knew the road where he was dropping me intersected with a major road that went back towards my home. I got out of the car and walked. I didn't consider, or care, that the walk would take about seven or eight hours to complete. Steve and my brother drove off, thinking I would shortly give in and beg them for a ride. Steve misjudged me.

I just started walking. At one point, in order to save some time and effort, I cut across a large parcel of undeveloped land. While I was cutting that corner, Steve and my brother drove back to where they thought I would be along the road. Of course, I was not there. Steve began to realize, I might very well walk all the way home. If I were allowed to do so, Steve would have some explaining to do to my parents. Steve and my brother began desperately driving back and forth along the road. Finally, they saw me. Steve commanded my brother to run out into the field to get me. I told my brother I was going to walk home. By this time, Steve had parked the car and came out into the field. My brother and I got into a fist fight. I lost. They forcefully escorted me back to the Lincoln Continental.

I doubt whether my brother had much choice in this matter. I certainly had no choice—that was apparent to me. If I resisted, I got beat up. I went along, but I buried my anger and resentment. It is quite obvious, in retrospect, I started to have my first bouts of depression when I was thirteen years old. I struggled sometimes with very deep depression all throughout my teenage years, and much of my adult life. Depression and Steve's Lincoln Continentals were constants in my life for many years.

In the early 1980s, I went completely public about my childhood sexual abuse at Steve's hands. I sued Steve. Well into the lawsuit process, but before the 1988 jury verdict against Steve, I was driving by his home in Minneapolis one afternoon. Parked in front of his home was a Lincoln Continental. Steve sat in the driver's seat. Sitting next to him was a boy, about twelve years old. Steve was talking. The boy was listening.

Knowing how Steve had held many such conversations with me, I became infuriated. I thought briefly about smashing my car into the driver's side of the Lincoln Continental. I thought of running up to Steve and assaulting him. I thought of yanking the boy out of the car and lecturing him on the dangers associated with Steve. But, I also thought how I might well completely lose control of myself in such a way that the police would arrive, then depart with me in handcuffs sitting in the back seat of a squad car, delighted to collar a crazed young lawyer.

I have long regretted that I did nothing to help that boy that day. Looking back at a time before I owned a cell phone, I might have gone to a nearby business and made a call to the police. But, even though the local police precinct knew Steve was a thief and a con artist, I doubt the police knew he was a pederast. Had the police arrived, Steve would merely have said, "What seems to be the problem, officer?"

After a few questions by the police, Steve would have said, "The boy? Yes. He does some odd jobs around the house a few days a week after school. I was just about to drive him home to his parents, who are expecting him soon for dinner."

The police would then have departed for, seemingly, more urgent business. After all, what is wrong or illegal about sitting in the front seat of a Lincoln Continental—a then almost sixty-year-old man sitting with a twelve-year-old boy? For that matter, what was wrong about his sitting with me several decades earlier in the front seat of a Lincoln Continental—a then thirty-seven-year-old man sitting with a twelve-year-old boy?

Several years after I started my lawsuit against Steve, but before the case went to trial in 1988, I met a man in his late twenties who had been molested as a youth. As an adult, he considered himself a gay man and a recovering alcoholic. In conversing with him, he told me how he had spent a recent Saturday with several friends on a boat trip hosted by an older, single man. As he described the man, the boat, the embarkation point, and the route traveled, my blood started to boil.

I probed his narrative with a few questions. *When did the trip begin?* (Early in the day.) *How long did it last?* (All day.) *Was there ever any opportunity for him to leave the boat, short of diving into the water and swimming to shore?* (No.) *Who else was on the trip?* (Several gay recovering *alcoholic* men.) *Was any alcohol available for the guests?* (Yes—provided by the host.) *Was the host a man in his mid-fifties?* (Yes.) *Did he have dark hair with a short haircut?* (Yes.) I asked one last question. I knew the answer even as I asked the question. *What was the host's name?* (Steve...something or other.)

In addition to targeting boys, Steve was now targeting vulnerable adult gay men. He had expanded his focus from boys to men; from *jail bait* to adult alcoholic gay males.

I told the young man, "You spent most of the day with a sociopath and pederast. He controlled the circumstances. He isolated you. He tempted all of you with alcohol. He was testing each of you to determine who was to be his next victim."

The young man became angry at me. He protested, "No, it was a pleasant afternoon with good friends and a warm and friendly host." Hearing his viewpoint, I toned down my outrage. But, based upon my own experience, I wondered what may have happened to the other men on the boat. Was Steve now using his forty-foot yacht as he had done with his Lincoln Continentals—as a tool for the isolation and grooming of more victims? I wondered whether this evil man could ever be stopped.

CHAPTER
NINE

Trained to Be Silent

Just as I was entering seventh grade, Steve and I were watching television at his home one Saturday evening. I believe it was an episode of *Bonanza*, during which the country doctor remarked to Ben Cartwright he had just attended a difficult birth elsewhere in the county—a breech birth. I turned and asked Steve, "What's a breech birth?" Seeing this as the golden opportunity he needed and had patiently awaited, he said, "Haven't your parents told you anything about *the birds and the bees*? What kind of parents are they? I am going to have a good talk with them. If they won't tell you about *the facts of life,* about sex, I guess I'll have to." Of course, I felt ashamed about my lack of knowledge, and doubly ashamed my parents hadn't told me. The effect was just as Steve intended.

The next Saturday evening I was at his home again. He reminded me about my previous week's question about a breech birth. He then told me he had talked with my parents. "Your parents are too uncomfortable to talk with you about sex," Steve told me. "Your parents asked me to explain the facts of life to you," Steve lied to me. So, Steve began his course of instruction. In the midst of this important instruction, and his demonstrating and touching, my pubescent body responded. He played with my body. I felt embarrassed, but I started to feel pleasure. What followed was new and both surprising and troubling to me. My childhood innocence came to an end, not gently and voluntarily given up to a peer, as is the case of most normal teenagers. My childhood innocence was stolen from me at the end of months of carefully planned seduction at the hands of a man three times my age.

As I look back on this, I do not actually recall all the details. I remember it occurred in a small bedroom located in the basement of the home in which he and his mother lived. Between the summer of 1963 and prior to her death in 1966, I had many sexual encounters with Steve in this room. It became a regular thing. What began as a once-a-week event fairly soon developed into a two- or three-times-a-week routine. During my later teenage years, the venue changed to many hotels and motels across the state and the nation. A couple times Steve joined me, my father, and my two older brothers on hunting trips. During those trips, Steve took particular joy in having sex with me within earshot of my family. Sometimes on these hunting trips, he molested me even in the same room as my father or my brothers, while they lay asleep!

One of the most curious things to me in retrospect was we never talked to each other about sex. Even when I was well beyond the age of consent, there was never any verbal communication between us as to likes or dislikes. There was never any planning discussions such as you might have with your wife or lover. We certainly never spoke about or discussed whether this conduct was illegal, immoral, or whether it was homosexual. He just engineered situations where we just did it. I complied. The topic of sex was surrounded by a wall of silence and denial. I now realize that if back then I could talk about it with him, there was a risk I would talk about it with others, thereby revealing Steve for what he was. He trained me to be silent.

The sexual release was pleasurable. This confused me a great deal. Here I was having sex with a man. I enjoyed the physical aspect of it up until my own climax. Once that happened, the tawdriness of it all, the guilt and shame of it all came tumbling down about me. At that moment, I was filled with disgust with what we had done. I felt disgust for myself. And yet this disgust was not so great that I didn't say, "No more!" until I was about twenty-five years old.

Through all those years from age twelve to age twenty-five, and for several years afterwards, I feared I was homosexual. Yet, all my sexual fantasies were heterosexual. I fell in love or had crushes on several women. I looked forward to the time I would be married, and have enjoyed being married for over a quarter century, now. Although I have been friends with several gay men over the years, I never engaged in sex with them or with any other male other than Steve. Yet, I feared I was a *homo* or a *queer*, as my then teenaged friends at school would have taunted.

One time in my early twenties when I was living at Steve's home, and working for him in his several businesses, a male friend of mine said to me as a cold, accusing statement of fact, "Mark, you are a homosexual."

"No, I am not!" I protested. What I did not realize at the time he made this observation, was Steve had molested him on at least one occasion. It occurred in the context of Steve giving him sex education!

If during junior high and high school, you asked me whether any of my friends and classmates were homosexual, I would have protested, "No. Of course not!" I did know two schoolmates who acted in a stereotypically *swishy* manner. But back then, I was so wrapped up in my own fear that my same-sex relationship with Steve might be discovered and I would be branded as homosexual, that it never even crossed my mind these schoolmates were gay. Several years after high school, I ran into one of these two schoolmates. He told me he was living in San Francisco with his partner. As he told me this, I thought, *You're gay!?! Well, of course you are.* He hadn't changed a bit. His sexual preferences just had never crossed my mind when we were in school together in the early 1960s. As for the other schoolmate, it had, likewise, never crossed my mind while we were teenagers that he might be gay. I was similarly shocked about him when one day I opened up the Minneapolis daily newspaper to the editorial/commentary page. Here was an opinion piece by him discussing how painfully lonely he had been as a closeted teenager, particularly at such times as homecoming and prom. As I read that article, I thought again, *You're gay!?! Well, of course you are.*

After graduating from high school, I went away to college in Massachusetts to attend Harvard University. While at college I had several friends and acquaintances who were gay. During my sophomore year I even worked on the set crew in a drag show that was the oldest theatrical company in America—the Hasty Pudding Theatricals. It was strange for me to have gay friends, while at the same time desperately hiding the fact I was in a sexual relationship with Steve.

The confusing thing about this was that I was not sexually attracted to these gay friends. I was curious about them, and, perhaps, titillated knowing about their life-style, but I never had any sexual feelings for them. In a certain regard, my friendships with these men were, simply, friendships.

In another regard, they were experiments testing whether I had any sexual attraction to men.

The most insane thing was that while I was away at Harvard, I had one life. I was heterosexual. Yet while I was back in Minneapolis, I lived another life at Steve's house, having a same-sex relationship with him.

Another example of my fear of being branded as gay happened when I was twenty-nine years old, and just prior to my marriage to my wife. We had a couple over for dinner at our apartment. As I was entertaining my friend's wife in the living room, my friend went into the kitchen to talk with my fiancee while she finished preparing our meal. My friend, as a ham-handed, practical joke, said to my fiancee, "Well, of course you know Mark is gay."

My fiancee nervously laughed it off, but a few minutes later, took me aside and repeated the conversation to me. (I had previously disclosed to my fiancee I had had a same-sex encounter at some time in my life, but that I was not homosexual.) When she told me what my friend had said, I lost my composure. Thinking Steve had told my friend I was gay in hopes the disclosure would upset and, perhaps, doom my pending marriage, or thinking my friend had somehow independently concluded I was gay, I marched into the living room and loudly confronted my friend and his wife.

"We have to get something quite clear if we are going to sit down and have dinner together. I don't know where you get your information. I do not know upon what facts you base your accusation. But, I am not gay!" I was so worked up, it is quite amazing we were able to continue our little dinner party and have a pleasant evening together.

My friend told me much later that on their drive home, after our dinner together, he said to his wife, "Man, the way Mark responded, I sure hit a mine field!" My friend, with his bizarre sense of humor, had no idea how big of a mine field he had stumbled into. This mine field was complicated. Three issues entwined together like the grapevines on a backyard arbor. One issue was simply teenaged conformity. Another issue was the confusion of homosexuality with pedophilia. Finally, there was the issue of how do we define manhood in our society.

I have watched my two children grow out of the delightful time between age eight and age thirteen. As teenagers, they both, of course, began the stage where they distanced themselves and separated from us, their parents. My teenagers *died a thousand deaths* when I dropped them off at school. God forbid their friends discover my children were even remotely connected to us, their parents. As a father, I gave advice to my teenagers endlessly. It was routinely ignored. Yet, given time to percolate, my teenagers came home and announced something as truth, just as certainly as if it had been received from the Oracle at Delphi, or if Moses had come down from the mountain with the advice engraved on a *stone* tablet. The advice was some authoritative and insightful advice offered by the posse, Tiffany-Caitlin-Sean-Brent-Michail-Dakota, via an *electronic* tablet. Along the same lines, to watch a gaggle of teenagers walk down the street was a hilarious event. Six or eight of them would skitter along in a tightly packed mob. Conformity to the peer group was paramount.

In the arena of sexuality, my teenagers were appalled at the thought that old people engaged in sex. The thought of same-sex relations between two people was doubly appalling. Combining the need for conformity with the disgusting thought of old people as sexual beings, how could I as a teenaged victim of childhood sexual abuse ever have dared broaching the issue with my friends? How could I have possibly mentioned my sexual relationship with a man who was so many years my senior?

As for the blurring of distinctions between homosexual relations between consenting adults, and same-sex pedophilic relations between an adult and a child, even today, most adults miss the point. One type of sexual encounter is between peers, the other is between the superior and the subservient. Likewise, most teenagers hold rigid views of appropriate sexual relations. There is no room in the teenager's mind for shades of gray. Sex between two men is, by definition, homosexual.

For most teenagers, the issue of same-sex relations does not conform. To not conform is to be different. To be different in the world of teenagers is the ultimate taboo. I was heterosexual, despite my secrets. Yet, as I was necking in some lovers' lane with my high school girlfriend in Steve's 1963 Buick Electra, how preposterous it would have been for me to say, "Oh! We have to stop. I have to bring you home by 11:00 so I can return the car to my uncle, and then spend the night at his house having sex with him."

The more global issue is critical. How do we define manhood in society? Certainly, appearances matter. When my son and daughter were little, I used to take them to my barber for their haircuts. One time, my then three-year-old daughter tried to cut her own hair. She really messed it up. It needed to be cut quite short, just to even up the cut all around her head. I instructed my barber, in his repair efforts, to trim the hair that covered my daughter's ears. My barber, without going into detail, asked, "Are you sure?"

I said, "Yes. Cut her hair fairly short, and cut the hair so that her ears show." For the next several weeks, people approached me when I was out shopping or playing in the park with my children, and commented, "You have such handsome boys!" Up until that haircut, I never realized women's hair almost always covers their ears. The most obvious exception to this unstated rule is when a woman is open about her lesbianism. In that case, a short haircut might be a badge of defiance or pride. *For a heterosexual teen-aged girl to show up school with a boy's haircut, you can be assured many of her peers will be thinking, rigidly, she must be gay.*

For a teenaged boy to look the least bit effeminate, or to act, as my two schoolmates from the 1960s did, with effeminate mannerisms, is to invite trouble from the rigid thinking of male peers. As a matter of fact, several years ago, I ran into yet another schoolmate from the 1960s. Back then, and even today, he cultivated a swagger when he walked. There was no doubt, here was a man, if you were to judge by the manner of his dress, his appearance, and his swagger. In catching up with him about several decades that had so swiftly passed, I asked if he was married. I also asked where he was living. He told me he was not married. He also told me he, for several years had been living in Provincetown, Massachusetts, but was soon to be moving to San Francisco. From this information, I made several assumptions. But, I dared not ask if he was gay. It didn't matter to me, other than as a matter of my own curiosity, and as a challenge to my own rigid thinking about how a man should act or dress. If he was gay, he certainly challenged my own stereotypical thinking about standard appearances.

For men, we have culturally conforming ideas about what is a man. Our media gives us examples such as John Wayne, Steve McQueen, Sean Connery, Harrison Ford, and, I suppose, Brad Pitt. During the 1950s and 1960s we also had role models in Tab Hunter, Rock Hudson, and Montgomery Clift over whom countless women, young and old, swooned. Yet, Tab, Rock, and Montgomery were gay!

For men, in our changing society, what qualities make up being a man? Is it still okay to be physically strong? What about strong and silent? Must a man still make more money than his wife? Dare a man stoop to the level of undertaking child-care tasks, such as changing a child's diaper or feeding a child? Where does a man, or a boy making the transition from boyhood to manhood, fit in, particularly in a society which increasingly is feminized?

Facing traditional beliefs about manhood, or the ever-changing and shifting sands of today's beliefs about manhood, how confusing it must be for a survivor of childhood sexual abuse. If he was abused by a man, as I was, to speak publicly about his experiences, risks being branded *a sissy or a wus.* If he was molested by a woman, when he was a child, for him to express fear or sadness about what was taken from him, is out of the question. His adult male peers would say to him, "You lucky stiff! I wish I had some older woman show me the ropes!" The male, having been so abused, may even come to deny his own feelings about the matter and readily join in with the locker room braggadocio.

Big boys don't cry! Show no weakness. When you hurt, suck it up and deny the pain. Win at all costs. He who makes the most money, or owns the most toys, wins. Score with as many women as possible. Drink the other guy under the table. Are these the standards by which a man's virility is judged?

Whether they make sense, or not, standards *are* standards. Society has certain views. Once you become a man, if the standards are clear-cut, you are a lucky man. Living up to the standards can thus be easy, *if* you are a man.

But what if you are a boy in a man's body? What if, when you were at a crucial developmental stage, you, as a boy, were raped? What if the cultural demands of our society, when you were, chronologically, a teenager, or now as a man, serve to lock that little boy in a psychological and emotional prison? Can you ever achieve manhood, if you are always separated from that imprisoned little boy? The boy who was not abused found ways to grow, psychologically, emotionally, and physically into a man. For the boy who was abused, how does he reintegrate the boy, the inner-child, with the stalking-horse impostor of a man he presents to the world today? Searching for the key to this dilemma was a heroic journey for me. Finding the key unlocked a great personal treasure trove.

CHAPTER TEN

The Nature of the Beast

Steve was a master of the tactic, divide and conquer. Isolating one party from the other in every way possible was the critical thing to do. His methods and stratagems were varied. But his efforts were relentless.

The home in which I spent the majority of my childhood was built of brick and was three stories tall. The third floor had two bedrooms and a full bath. At first my two older brothers lived up there. When the eldest graduated from high school and moved out to join the U.S. Navy, I moved upstairs from my second floor bedroom to one of the third floor bedrooms. My next older brother occupied the other bedroom until he graduated from high school and also enlisted in the U.S. Navy.

My mother was what is now termed a "stay-at-home" mom. Back then, she was, simply, a mother and housewife. As part of her daily routine, mother got up early to fix father his breakfast. As he went off to work, she yelled to us children, "Rise and shine." Every morning we danced the same dance of most every household. While she cooked breakfast and set the kitchen table, she warned, "Hurry up! Breakfast is on the table. You'll be late for school." These broadcasts were met with, "I'm hurrying! I'll be down in a minute. I am hurrying as fast as I can, but I can't find my homework assignment."

Beginning in 1963, Steve came by our house most school day mornings. He came upstairs between 6:00 and 6:30 a.m. He first visited my brother in his room and then he visited me in my room. Afterwards, he ate breakfast with our family. Then, for my mother's benefit, he played on the electric organ in the living room, old favorite songs from the 1920s, 1930s, and 1940s. He then drove us to school—my brother to high school and me to junior high school.

When my mother called upstairs to us, she yelled from the kitchen up through the stairwell. But if the door between the second floor landing and the third floor stairway was closed, we could not hear her and she could not hear our replies. She then came to the second floor, opened the door to the third floor stairwell, and yelled to my brother and me. There was always a risk she might ascend the third floor stairway and come up to our bedrooms. Had she done this, she would have found Steve in bed with my brother, or in bed with me.

One day, in an ever so helpful manner, Steve said to my mother, " I hate to have you running up and down the stairs in the morning. You know, it wouldn't take much effort to wire an intercom up through the abandoned laundry chute from the kitchen up to the third floor." My mother replied, "Oh, that would be awfully expensive to get an electrician in here to wire it. It just isn't in the budget."

Steve then offered, "I can buy an intercom system at wholesale. I will be glad to install it for you at no cost."

How could my mother turn down such a deal? She must have thought, *That Steve! How could we get along without him. He is so generous and so helpful. And he takes such a genuine interest in our boys!* The idea of an intercom seemed fantastic. My mother said, "Okay. When can it be done?"

Steve said, "I'll get on it right away! I know you will be pleased with the convenience of having an intercom."

Thereafter, my brother and I, *and* Steve, heard my mother's entreaties to get moving *not* from the second floor stair landing, but from the tinny sounding intercom speaker mounted just outside our third floor bedroom doors. When we...*when Steve*...heard my mother's voice from that speaker, we each knew mother was in the kitchen, two flights of stairs away and not standing in our bedroom doorway. Oh! The wonders of the electronic age. Electronics make our lives so much more productive.

Physical isolation was one of his tricks. So was interpersonal isolation.

One of Steve's businesses was a service station and automotive garage. Over the years, Steve owned many cars. Sometimes he bought a car from a customer who had grown tired of paying for repairs. Steve had his mechanics fix the car and put it in tip-top shape. Steve then drove it for a few months and later re-sold it. On occasion, he sold a car to our family.

One particular car I remember was a beautiful blue Mercury Park Lane sedan. It had lots of chrome trim, white leather upholstery, front bucket seats, electric windows, automatic door locks, air conditioning, a really nice sounding radio, and wonder of wonders—an eight-track stereo tape player! While Steve owned it, he took me on a long spring vacation trip to Florida. Since I had my learner's driving permit, Steve let me drive this car a great many miles during that vacation. At some time after that trip, Steve sold this car to my father. Since I was so familiar with that car, it really pleased me my father bought it from Steve.

During my sophomore year in high school I passed my driver's test and got my driver's license. About this time, I fell madly in love with a visiting foreign student from Sweden. She did not return my love, but she was happy to let me take her out to dinner and a movie most every Friday night during the months she and her family lived in Minneapolis. I wanted to be with her and, typical of a teenaged male, to impress her with the fine car my father now owned.

On one date, we went to a play at a local private girls' school. As it happened, I was a member of the cast of the school's production of Edgar Lee Master's *Spoon River Anthology*. The play went well. My date enjoyed watching the show. We walked out to the car after the show. I held the car door open for her. I went around to the driver's side of the car and got in. I started the car. As I put the car into reverse, my date's hand accidentally brushed up against my leg as she buckled her seat belt. My cautious and sedate backing out of the parking space immediately became rather more spirited than I intended. Hormones and pent up frustration! My father's beautiful Mercury sedan sailed across the parking lot right into a telephone pole, smashing the left rear taillights. Embarrassment and shame filled my heart. Worry over my father's possible reaction soon followed.

After taking my date home, I drove over to Steve's and showed him the damage. "Your father is not going to like this," he warned.

"What can be done?" I asked.

"Don't worry! Leave the car with me. I'll have my mechanics fix it tomorrow," he said. He gave me one of his other cars to drive home. He counseled me on what lie to tell my father. He later called my father to back up the lie. Steve returned the Mercury to my father a day, or so, later—taillight and body work all taken care of.

Looking back at things, my father would not have gone into a rage. He would have laughed at what happened and told me I would have to pay for the repairs out of my wages. But I believed Steve's dire warnings, not realizing his agenda. In agreeing on a cover story and having Steve take care of the repairs, he drove a wedge between my father and me. I was indebted to Steve. The car repair problem was solved, but at a great cost. Now, I had yet one more thing to be silent about.

To really control my life, Steve needed to control my sources of income. Steve hatched a clever scheme that deprived me of income from my first *real* job, made my parents look evil to me, and played upon my fears surrounding the issue of homosexuality.

Steve sensed my fear of being labeled gay, even as he continued to engage me in same-sex relations. In our society, despite the changes of the past few decades, for a heterosexual teenager or, for that matter, a grown man, to be falsely labeled as gay is very disturbing to him. If he is gay, but closeted, it is also disturbing. I think, at its core, the label is one that brings into question one's manhood. It is also a label that means you are different. For a teenage boy, whose ideas of his own masculinity, and of manhood in general, are just forming, such a label is painful, maddening, and humiliating. For a teenager, the label is one that says *you don't fit in with the pack*. This brand of being different from other teenagers sears the heart and soul.

Steve played on my fears in this arena. One time when I was fourteen or fifteen years old, Steve took me to New York City to see the sights and to see several Broadway plays. At one theater, while the audience awaited the curtain to rise, Steve pointed out a middle-aged male couple who appeared to me to be gay by their stereotypic manner of dress and affectation. Steve asked me, "Well, Mark, do you suppose you will grow up to look and act like them?" I simply shuddered at that prospect. Steve enjoyed seeing me squirm with disgust and revulsion. I was so consumed by the shame of my sexual relationship with Steve. As is the case for many people, I also was confusing the issue of his pedophilia with the very different issue of homosexuality. Most of all, I was so much into denial about things, I couldn't bear to even discuss these confusing issues openly. Steve still enjoyed seeing me in pain. He enjoyed inflicting it.

As an adult, I enjoy attending the theater with my wife and two children. As our children get older, it has been fun to discuss the plot, the character development, the actors' skill, and other topics. I really enjoyed the theater as a teenager.

When I was sixteen years old, I landed the perfect job. My first *real* job. I quit my morning newspaper route and became an usher at the Minneapolis Guthrie Theater, our renowned dramatic repertory stage. I was happy and proud of this. Not only could I earn spending money, but I could watch the plays when not busy with my duties as an usher. I was following my bliss.

Such a healthy and remunerative pursuit was at odds with Steve's overall long term plan for me. He wanted me to work for him, and to, ultimately, completely depend upon him. Having an independent source of income and doing a job I loved, working for someone else, just wouldn't do.

Steve took me aside one day and told me, "You know, your parents really don't like that you are an usher in the theater. In fact, they are dead set against it. I tried to reason with them. But you know how parents can be."

I asked, "Why are they against my doing a job that I love?"

"Because you are working in the theater, and everybody knows the theater is a haven for homosexuals."

"I didn't know that. But nobody has bothered me," I protested.

Steve said, "What matters is what they might do to you. The long and the short of it is your parents insist you quit your job as an usher."

To even have this conversation with the man who molested me was so bizarre. My mind was so divided and fractured, I couldn't even contemplate its absurdity. With much anger in my heart towards what was supposedly my parents' viewpoint and their final decision in the matter, I quit working as an usher. Of course, I never bothered to confirm with them anything Steve had alleged.

But I still needed spending money. Who do you suppose just happened to have an opening at his business? Steve.

When Steve recounted the facts about something, what somebody said, or what had been decided, his narrative contained a great many falsehoods that were slanted in his favor. The narrative held just enough truth, however, to make its overall truthfulness believable. In my youthful shame and guilt, I could not discern the veracity of any of Steve's statements. On this he depended. On this I suffered. Ironically, in my high school math class we studied mathematical logic. One of the first rules we learned was *a true statement plus a false statement equals a false conclusion!*

To cut me loose from all family moorings, Steve had to engineer an even greater crisis between me and my parents. Often you read about how pimps gain control over the women they prostitute. There is the great seduction, the great push to gain the affections and the devotion of the *girl.* There are the kind words, a great many gifts, and many meals in nice restaurants. Sometimes there are trips to places she has long dreamed of visiting. But somewhere along the way, the pimp must engineer the *crisis* with the girl's family. The girl is given the choice of staying in her family's fold, which is usually troubled in some way. The trouble in her family may be divorce; drunkenness; or physical, sexual, or emotional abuse. Most any other living arrangement looks preferable to her. When the crisis comes, often the family members—father or mother—attempt to re-assert their authority over the young woman. But that authority was lost long ago. She, following clumsy scripts of so many families and so many eras, leaves. In her mind, she is asserting her independence. In her family's eyes, she is making a great mistake. The lines are sharply drawn.

The pimp deftly engineers this very moment when he says, "Why don't you move in with me? I will take care of you." The young woman, desperate for approval, happily agrees, not knowing she is signing her psychological and emotional death warrant. She leaves her family, walks out the door thinking she is getting into a royal carriage drawn by many beautiful horses. She thinks she is finally free and independent, generously supplied by her handsome prince.

In fact, when she walks out that door, she is walking a gangplank. She is exchanging a difficult situation for a terrible one. Her pimp will now become her jailer and taskmaster. The shackles are locked onto her ankles. She now does her jailer's bidding. Now, when she no longer has any means of emotional or psychological support, the pimp forces the cruelest of circumstances upon her. She has nowhere else to turn. Even if she has some insight, she is drained of her will to make positive changes in her life.

Steve didn't prostitute me to others. Instead, I became *his* very own prostitute. Over time, I became almost a robot, an automaton. But Steve engineered the pimp-prostitute crisis between me and my parents, especially between me and my mother. At the beginning of my senior year in high school, I moved from my family home to Steve's home.

My bewildered and frustrated parents sought Steve's counsel throughout these years. *What was the matter with Mark? Why does he sulk so? Why is he so difficult? Why did he move out?*

My mother was particularly devastated by my move to Steve's home. While I triumphed in escaping her, my mother shed many tears. At the time, she desperately implored my father, "What have we done? Why did he feel compelled to move out? How can we ever win our son back?"

My father, whose own mother had orchestrated every aspect of his young life, and against whom he rebelled by marrying my mother, could only recite a nursery rhyme platitude to my sobbing mother, "Leave him alone, and he'll come home, wagging his tail behind him."

Although we didn't realize it at the time, my parents and I were a pitiful match for Steve and his schemes. It took us all years to finally see the light. For years, I tried to sort it all out—the truth from the lies. I finally could only achieve a measure of sanity when I simply assumed that anything and everything Steve ever told me was a lie. Sometimes, I doubted even this judgment. My judgment was, fortunately, affirmed by a little piece of paper that came to light many years later.

I reviewed some old files of mine in our basement, trying to weed out old receipts, canceled checks, bank statements, and other detritus of modern legal and economic life. I came across an old psychological test, a Minnesota Multi-Phasic Inventory (MMPI) report about Steve. I obtained this report when I was in the process of suing Steve for his molesting me as a child.

Steve, in cultivating me as one of his victims, skillfully held himself out to be a mature, moral adult who could be trusted and who really cared for me as a young man. In my youthful innocence, because of my *father hunger*, and in my need for love, affection, and approval, I believed him.

The report told otherwise:

> The results of the test taken by the subject are technically invalid because of extreme defensiveness and denial of shortcomings, which borders on deliberate distortion. Subject tends to give socially approved answers about himself regarding self control and moral values; the results of the test should be interpreted with caution. This pattern of test responses is frequently associated, how-

> ever, with socially immature and demanding individuals who have little to offer in the way of support and understanding to others and equally as little insight into their own functioning. An accurate picture of subject's personality and functioning is sufficiently concealed by his guardedness that a statement about possible sexual maladjustment cannot be made. There are no signs of an ongoing psychotic process. I would expect subject to be a highly manipulative individual with an elaborate system of rationalizations and denial for inappropriate behavior.

I can almost hear Steve saying, "Oh! That MMPI test was such a joke! The questions in it were simply ridiculous. How can a test really measure the character of a man, anyway? You have known me for many years. You should trust your own good judgment. Besides, everybody knows most psychologists and psychiatrists go into that profession because they are half crazy in the first place! How could one of their tests be at all reliable?"

If only I had seen Steve's MMPI report in 1963. If only my parents had seen this MMPI report at any time during my teens and had seen and understood its ramifications. Would we have acted upon it, or would we have been lulled to sleep by Steve's portrayal of it? I wonder.

What was he? Sociopath? Psychopath? Viper? Scorpion?

For many years, I felt incredible anger and indignation towards Steve. I wondered: *How could anybody be so selfish? Why didn't he have any feelings of consideration towards those around him? How could he be so hurtful? Why was he so manipulative? Why was he so evil?*

Re-reading Steve's MMPI gave me some perspective on the matter. Running across an ancient story, sometimes attributed to Aesop, helped me understand the situation more clearly. The story is *The Scorpion and the Frog*.

> One day a scorpion came upon a frog who, on the banks of a wide river, was basking himself in the warm afternoon sun. The scorpion, for reasons of his own, wanted to get across the river, but he could not swim. The scorpion awakened the frog and in a sickeningly courteous manner asked him, "Would you please transport me across the river, Mr. Frog?"

The startled frog stood ready to leap to safety because the frog knew he could be killed by the scorpion's sting. "Mr. Scorpion, how do I know you will not kill me while I am transporting you?"

"Don't be silly! If I were to kill you, I, as your passenger, would drown as you sank to the bottom of the river," replied the scorpion.

The frog asked, "Mr. Scorpion, how do I know you won't kill me once we reach the other riverbank?"

The scorpion assured the frog in his sweetest, most convincing voice, "I would not kill you because I would be so terribly grateful to you and indebted to you for having carried me across the river!"

The frog therefore agreed to ferry the scorpion across the river. The scorpion mounted the frog's back. Together, they entered the river, but the frog was soon in for a great surprise. Half way across the river, the scorpion stung the frog. The venom quickly affected the frog. Mr. Frog felt his legs and then his entire body go numb. He knew he would soon sink to the river's bottom.

"Mr. Scorpion, you promised my safety. Why have you stung me? Don't you realize when I succumb to your poison, I will drown—-and your death will soon follow?"

Mr. Scorpion replied, " I am sorry!—Well, actually, I am not sorry. I am just saying that."

Mr. Frog implored, "Then why did you do it?"

The scorpion reconsidered and then replied, "It is simply my nature."

Steve was the scorpion. My family and I were his frogs.

CHAPTER

ELEVEN

One Brick at a Time

Steve was not content to have me merely as his sexual boy-toy. He had to separate me from my family so that I became completely dependent upon him. Furthermore, he had to bind me with shame and guilt by involving me in his criminal schemes.

The earliest crime he involved me in was the theft of a car bumper. Steve had given or sold to my brother a 1956 blue Pontiac. It was my brother's first car, but it was missing its front bumper. One Saturday night Steve, an old friend of Steve's, my brother, and I drove out in the country to a farm Steve had previously scouted out. In a field not far from the farmhouse sat a 1956 Pontiac, the same model as my brother's car. Of course, this Pontiac had a front bumper. Steve, his old friend, my brother, and I got out of Steve's Lincoln Continental. Steve, his friend, and my brother took a large tarp, a few tools, and a portable acetylene torch out of the car trunk. They carefully spread the tarp over the car, draping it in such a way as to mask the bright light of the acetylene torch they intended using. Steve's friend then took the acetylene torch, crawled under the farmer's old junked Pontiac, ignited the torch, and cut the old rusty bolts that held the Pontiac's bumper to the car chassis. While Steve's friend quietly packed up the tools and the tarp, Steve and my brother lifted the detached bumper into the trunk of the Lincoln Continental. We all got into the car and quietly drove off.

During this entire affair, I was told to remain silent and stand by the car, but not to worry. Steve told me, "The farmer gave me permission to take the bumper off this old Pontiac." I followed these instructions obediently. I was so young and naive, it didn't even cross my mind that I was watching and passively participating in the car bumper's theft.

One of Steve's long term goals was to drag me down to his level. Up until meeting Steve, and since escaping his control, I followed the straight and narrow path. I had, and still have, clear cut ideas about what is right and what is wrong. In contrast to this, Steve was a horribly corrupt man. He sought to corrupt those around him. His gift giving was one example of a sort of corruption. In my case, having me accompany him while he did something illegal was the first stage of corrupting me. The car bumper theft was an initiation rite. I played Oliver Twist to Steve's well rehearsed Fagin.

The first clear cut example of corrupting me that I remember involved the soft drink machine at Steve's business. Sometimes I rode my bicycle home from junior high school. Steve's business was only a few blocks away from my school. I stopped by. He came out to talk with me. He asked me "Would you like to make some really good money?"

I replied, "How much is good money?"

He said, "Ten bucks, maybe more." This amount of money was a large amount to me. On my morning paper route, I worked for about an hour each day and usually cleared less than a dollar for that day. Ten or more dollars. Wow!

I said, "Okay. What do I have to do?" Steve handed me some small change and instructed me to buy myself a soft drink from the machine, making sure I leaned my bicycle against it while doing so. That seemed silly, but easy enough. So I did it. My strict upbringing and my ideas of right and wrong didn't seem compromised.

Steve then said, "Now, I am going to report to the soft drink distributor, the owner of the machine, that you came by today, bought a soft drink, and received an electric shock from the machine." That didn't seem right to me. I protested a bit. Steve said for the first of many times during the next decade, "Don't worry. You won't get into trouble. If any trouble arises, I will take responsibility. Just go along with me on this one."

So, I reluctantly said, "Well, okay."

A few days later, Steve handed me a crisp new twenty dollar bill. "I talked with the pop distributor and their insurance agent. They paid this money so you wouldn't sue them," Steve falsely claimed. I foolishly and unwittingly took the twenty dollars. At age thirteen, I thus sold my soul to the devil's agent. Steve succeeded in simply and clearly corrupting me. Apart from the shame of his sexual abuse of me, Steve now had something else to hold over me to keep me silent. It was just one small brick in a wall that he would skillfully build around me isolating me from my family and, now, the world.

From fairly early on, I accompanied Steve and my brother on some other outings, sometimes reluctantly, sometimes willingly. These did not seem extraordinary, but as I look back, several served to introduce me further to Steve's criminal life.

Steve had a couple of small businesses during the years he dominated my life. One of his businesses was a heating and air conditioning mechanical contracting company. In this business, he installed and repaired boilers, furnaces, and air conditioning systems. He worked for numerous commercial businesses and warehouses. Because heating and air conditioning systems can fail or malfunction any time, day or night, Steve was entrusted with keys to several of his customers' buildings.

My older brother or I accompanied Steve on legitimate service calls to repair a business's heating or air conditioning system. We fetched pliers or screwdrivers, or held a flashlight. We were gophers. *Go for this. Go for that.*

Sometimes we went to these businesses with Steve and it wasn't a service call. For instance, when I was in junior high school, I was assigned a project where I planted and tended my own small garden plot. When I told Steve, he said, "Well, you will want to protect your plants from rabbits." I wondered how would I do that. Late one Saturday evening, Steve, my brother, and I went to a downtown building supply warehouse to which Steve had a key. While there, at Steve's suggestion, we gathered up fencing, some metal fence posts, and some baling wire. I asked Steve, "Is it okay for us to be here after hours picking up supplies?"

Steve replied, "Yes. Don't worry about it. I have an account here. I will call the business office on Monday morning and give them a list of the things we pick up tonight." This sounded plausible to me. But in this particular case, something odd happened that undercut Steve's assurances to me. While we were in the warehouse, we went into the office area for some reason. At that moment, by pure coincidence, an automatic fire sprinkler head failed. The sprinkler head began spraying the office with water. Steve, stunned for a moment, quickly realized the fire and police department would respond to the apparent fire within about five or six minutes. He yelled at my brother and me to run, with the collected supplies, to the car parked out back. He followed us close behind. We all got into the car and sped out of the parking lot. When we were a block or two away, we heard and then saw four or five fire trucks and a couple police cars responding to the false alarm caused by the malfunctioning sprinkler system.

Steve was greatly relieved we were not caught in the warehouse. Looking back on things, I don't recall what song and dance Steve engaged in to convince me we were in the warehouse legitimately and not as burglars. It wasn't until many years later that I clearly realized we were in that warehouse committing a crime.

Steve even felt compelled to indirectly involve my father in Steve's corrupt schemes. Our family lived in an old house. After a long day at work, my father came home, read the daily newspaper, and supped with us. During the summer months, he went outside to strip the paint from all the exterior window trim, before repainting. In the course of the summer, he refurbished all the windows on one side of the house. During the winter months, he attended to other projects inside the house.

One project was replumbing the entire house. Our house was built in the early 1900s. The water pipes in the house were made of galvanized iron. Over the years, these pipes clogged up such that minerals coated the entire inside length of every pipe, somewhat like cholesterol can lead to the narrowing of your body's arteries. Water still flowed through the pipes at a reduced pressure. But if you took a shower in one part of the house when someone flushed the toilet or turned on the garden hose, the water in the shower swiftly slowed to a dismal trickle. My father decided to remedy this by replumbing the house with copper pipes.

Then, as now, you needed a building permit to do such work. Back then, though, things such as plumbing could only be done by a licensed plumber. My father decided he could not afford a licensed plumber. So at Steve's suggestion he did not take out a permit and he did not hire a licensed plumber. He chose to do it himself, with Steve's help and instruction. Back then I don't think you could get many plumbing supplies as readily as you can today. The house needed more than a hundred feet of copper pipe and many copper fittings. Where could my father turn for supplies?

As a building contractor, Steve bought plumbing supplies at wholesale. So Steve obtained the copper pipe and the fittings for my father to replumb the house. I am sure Steve charged my father for the supplies. Or, he said, "Oh, you don't need to pay me for these supplies. I ordered too many when I did the last commercial plumbing job. I need to get rid of the excess supplies." If Steve said and did this, it was to further make my father feel indebted to him.

Where did the plumbing supplies actually come from? Years later, I learned that Steve stole the supplies from the same warehouse where we obtained my garden fencing supplies. Had my father known the truth back then, he would have been absolutely mortified. Had my father been prosecuted for receiving stolen property from Steve, the mortification would have been extreme.

When Steve wanted something. He sometimes bought it at legitimate, but bargain prices. If he couldn't get it from somebody legitimately, he swindled them out of it. If he couldn't swindle them out of it, he stole it from them. Steve's code was completely at odds with my father's code, and the code by which I was raised. My father was an exceedingly honest and forthright man. Steve was a sociopath—exceedingly dishonest and devious. The most amazing thing about Steve was that if you caught him *red handed* or *dead to rights* he talked his way out of it. He just did not care about how anybody else, or society, viewed things. He viewed the world, and the people in it, as objects to be moved about, without concern for their own well-being. Certainly he had no concern for the niceties of the law, morality, or truth.

As Steve got older, he involved himself less with outright burglary or theft. Over the time he dominated me, he graduated into more paper crimes, white collar crimes. Steve once related to me the advice he got from his convicted embezzler father on one of the few times during Steve's life when they were together. Steve's father advised him, "You can make far more money with the stroke of a pen than you can with the sweat of your brow." Steve took this fatherly, and sociopathic, advice to heart.

When I was fifteen, Steve tried to enlist my help in testing his father's motto. Again, I was a game piece being moved around Steve's little chessboard without knowing the import of each move.

Our state offers a reduced real estate tax rate on our homes. If you live in the home as of January 2nd of a particular year you could get reduced homestead real estate taxes the following year. To get the reduced rate, you had to file a certain document with the city assessor every year. The home Steve lived in was owned by his mother. Prior to her death, Steve's mother properly filed for this reduced homestead tax classification every year. She died in 1966 and therefore on January 2nd of 1967, couldn't file for homestead tax status for taxes due in 1968. But Steve wanted to keep the reduced tax status, so he forged her name on the city assessor's required document. At the time, I didn't know these requirements, nor did I know he forged her signature.

One day, he drove me downtown to city hall, handed me a piece of paper, and instructed me to go up to a certain room to deliver this piece of paper for filing with the city assessor. I did as I was told. The clerk looked at the piece of paper supposedly signed by Steve's mother and she said to me, "Why, my goodness. This woman was my English teacher in high school many years ago. She couldn't still be alive, could she?"

I replied quite frankly and innocently, "No, she died several months back." I then returned to Steve who was driving his car around the block. I related to him what the clerk said, and what I replied. Steve went into a fit. "Why did I have to be such a blabbermouth?" he yelled.

It is a crime to falsely file for homestead status or to forge another person's signature. Steve knew this, but he committed the crimes, nevertheless. He also involved me, without my knowing, in his little criminal scheme. Steve was lucky the clerk did not refer the matter to the police for prosecution. Her office simply denied the homestead tax classification, and the hoped-for reduction in real estate taxes.

What should Steve have done? He was an only child of his divorced mother. He, therefore, was her sole heir. The house should have gone to him, if she had died without having a will or had she died with a will naming him as the sole beneficiary. But the law required that the title be probated in order to place Steve in legal title to the home. Since probate cost additional money for filing fees and attorney's fees, Steve took another course of action. He went to a stationery store and bought a blank warranty deed form. He drew up a back-dated deed supposedly conveying the home from his mother to himself. He forged his deceased mother's signature. He even forged the notary public's signature notarizing the deed.

Many years later when, as a real estate lawyer, I investigated the title to this home. In examining the microfilmed warranty deed on file at the county real estate records office, I noticed the standard deed form used by Steve did not even exist during his mother's life. The deed forms had been redesigned by the state legislature a few years *after* his mother's death. Secondly, the deed had been notarized by a local druggist, who was dead by the date the warranty deed supposedly had been signed by Steve's mother.

What incredible nerve! But like the scorpion, it was just in Steve's nature. Not only that, but he came by his criminal nature quite naturally, from his convicted embezzler father. I did *not* come by crime naturally. I had to be persuaded, cajoled, threatened, and trained by Steve.

My parents were very devout, highly ethical people. Lying, stealing, and bearing false witness—each part of the Ten Commandments—were not a part of their repertoire. These things were simply wrong. In addition, at least in my father's case, he knew from life experience violating these Biblical commandments just was not an effective life strategy. Somehow, if you violated these commandments, life eventually, and justly, punished you.

My father told me of a childhood event illustrating this. As a boy of ten or eleven, back in the 1920s, he stole a dollar or two in change from his father's dresser. With this money, he went out and bought a brand new baseball mitt. He proudly brought it home from the sporting goods store. As he walked down the country road towards his home, he tossed his baseball up in the air and happily caught it in his fantastic new mitt. As he was just about to walk up the driveway of his home, he realized his mother's first question when he walked in the door would be, "Earl, that's a lovely new baseball mitt. Just where did you get the money to buy such a fine thing?" He did not have a satisfactory answer to this likely question. So, my father carefully hid the new mitt under some brush by their roadside mailbox. The next morning, my father went out to the roadside to retrieve his new baseball mitt from under the brush. During the night, either his parents found the mitt, or somebody else found the mitt my father had purchased with stolen money! In either case, it was gone. Of course, circumstances created by my father prevented him from ever mentioning the missing baseball mitt to his parents.

My parents believed most people were good people. In their dealings with people, they assumed other people were ethical and trustworthy, until proven otherwise. Even holding this belief, my father also allowed for people's *private* foibles. My father told me another story about a very close friend of his. This friend was a highly successful, mechanically oriented man, who had built a highly profitable business, despite his having only a high school education. With his wealth, this man, a married man, took up a mistress. My parents often socialized with this man and his wife, but my father's friend also wanted my parents to socialize with him and his mistress. My father told his friend, "You know I value your friendship. I have turned a blind eye towards your *private* affairs. But, for you to ask me to *publicly* socialize with you and your mistress, while I am still friends with your wife, is asking me to put a stamp of approval upon your philandering. I can't and won't do that." My father's friend never pressed the issue with my father again.

The most significant error my parents committed in believing people were good directly affected me. When my next older brother was in high school and I was in junior high school, my cousin Gene, from across town, revealed to his mother and to another of my mother's older sisters that Steve had molested him. My two aunts held a meeting to decide what to do about this revelation. My aunts spoke with my parents about the allegation. My parents were quite concerned. They talked with my next older brother, laid out the case, and, no doubt, filled with fear and dread, desperately asked/told him, "Tell us! Steve isn't molesting you, too?"

My brother, one of Steve's victims, wanting to accommodate my parents, in some manner protect me, and also avoid a great deal of explanation and personal embarrassment for himself, answered, "No, Steve isn't molesting me." This, of course, was the answer my parents wanted and needed to hear, and believe. But, they never took the time to ask me about it. In shame, I might have lied. Maybe my parents would have seen the lie in my demeanor and would have inquired further and taken action to protect me. But, the reality, the truth, was too much for them to accept or bear.

My parents persisted in believing Steve was the kind, generous, helpful bachelor who expressed his unmet desire to be a parent to us boys by spending so much time with us. As for my cousin Gene, my parents concluded, if Steve had actually done such a heinous act to him, why did Gene continue in Steve's employ?

Many years later, when I was just going public with the facts of my abuse, my father and mother came to my wife's and my apartment from their new home in South Dakota. My father said to me, "As long as we are in town, I ought to go over to Steve's house to visit." My father and mother's faith in the essential goodness of Steve was then put to a shattering test.

I took a deep breath and said, "Dad, there are some things about Steve I need to discuss with you...." My process of unburdening deeply burdened my parents. At one point, my reticent father turned to my mother, in private, and wailed, "What have we done to our kids?"

However much my disclosures burdened my parents, the process was a significant step toward reintegrating my fractured life. From the time I was first molested by Steve, I began living a double life. As time passed, my double life became increasingly complex and layered with ever deeper layers of illegal and immoral conduct under Steve's direction and influence. What was so hard for me to understand was that I was cut from the same cloth as my father, both in my need to be truthful and forthright, and my later need to desperately keep the lid on my troubles. Innately, I was very rigid in my living and in telling the truth. As a boy, I voraciously read biographies of the great men of American history. I particularly admired Abraham Lincoln. I remember being profoundly struck by the story of how Honest Abe walked several miles from his frontier store to return some small change accidentally left behind by one of his customers.

An example of my personal honesty, prior to Steve's involvement in my life, arose during my third grade class spelling bee. The whole class participated. Each student was eliminated, in turn, with their misspellings. It was finally down to the three bookworms of the class, Gretchen, Paula, and me.

The tie-breaking word next given to us was *Wednesday*. I was up first. I didn't know how to spell the word. I knew its spelling was tricky. I knew it was spelled differently than we pronounced it—WENDS-DAY. More importantly, I also knew if I simply glanced a little to the left of my two opponents, I could read the correct spelling from the top of our class calendar. I knew I could do this, but I knew to do so would be wrong. So, I looked straight at my teacher, knowingly misspelled the word the way it sounded, and resigned myself to accepting third place.

There was nobility within me. Several years later, I met and contended with Steve's very real and substantial ignobility. In that challenge of several years later, Steve felt compelled to corrosively destroy the latent nobility and goodness within me. I struggled with him, but in my relative youth and naivete, I could not overcome the evil machinations of a man, so many years my senior.

Shakespeare dramatically portrayed a similar relationship in the play *Henry IV.* The noble, young Prince Hal wasted his youth in the company of a huge, rotund man, many years his senior, who was a known thief, braggart, and drunkard. This man was Falstaff. The longer their relationship went on, the more compliant Prince Hal became. Falstaff began to bank upon his own prospects when the young Prince Hal would ascend the throne of his father and become Henry V. In this struggle between personal good and evil, between the corrupt Falstaff and the latently and innately, true and honest Prince Hal, something had to awaken the prince to his royal duties.

My first name is Mark, which means *warrior*. My middle name, Earl, was my father's first name. It means *noble.* To what depths would I, the *noble warrior* descend under the tutelage of my own Falstaff, Steve? To redeem me, what mantle of sovereignty could some day be placed upon *my* shoulders to remind *me* of my duties to myself and to society? When would *I* achieve sovereignty over *myself*? When and under what circumstances would *I* put Steve aside, as Prince Hal did to Falstaff upon the prince's coronation as king of England?

Many years after that third grade spelling bee, my mantle would be a red tie, a white shirt, and a blue dress suit, as well as the flags of the United States of America and the State of Minnesota. My coronation would be my swearing in ceremony as a newly minted attorney at law. My sovereignty would flow, in part, from that new status. My duty would no longer be a slavish duty to Steve, but a proud duty to our society and to the law. My sword and shield would be justice and the law.

The law would render justice to Steve, but not to his liking.

CHAPTER TWELVE

The Blinders Come Off

I moved from my family home to Steve's house in the beginning of my senior year in high school. Within my little high school world, I was at the top of my game. I was a member of the student council. I was senior class president. I spent part of the previous summer as my high school's representative to the American Legion's Boys' State. I was an Eagle Scout and a leader of my boy scout troop. My grades in school were excellent. I was elected to the National Honor Society. Later in my senior year, I performed in the senior class play. By the end of my senior year, I applied to and was accepted by Harvard University. To pay for such an expensive college, I applied for and was awarded a full four-year U.S. Navy ROTC scholarship worth thousands of dollars.

Steve was also at the top of his game. Over several years, he had groomed me, isolated me, molested me, overcome my emotional and psychological resistance to him, converted me into his most loyal supporter, fended off family charges that he had molested my cousin Gene, engineered a crisis between me and my family, and arranged for my move to his home.

The fly in the ointment for Steve, after such masterful gains over me, was that the next fall I would leave for Harvard. With my Navy ROTC scholarship, I would also be undergoing military training every summer between my years at Harvard. At the end of four years at Harvard, I would then become a second lieutenant in the U.S. Navy and serve it for up to seven years. Steve's prize was about to leave his control and domination.

Lucky for Steve, in the spring of 1969, the college campuses of the nation erupted in anti-war chaos. The radicals at Harvard ousted the ROTC programs from Harvard. So, only a couple weeks after I received the coveted acceptance letter from Harvard, and after being awarded my Navy ROTC scholarship, I was without my scholarship and could not pay for the huge expenses of attending Harvard. To replace the lost scholarship money, I couldn't get any financial aid from Harvard because it considered my family to be too well off. To make matters worse, my father refused to pay more than the cost of attending the University of Minnesota. In short, Harvard wanted the then unattainable sum of $8,000 per year for tuition, room, and board. My father would only pay $1,500. How was I to make up the difference in order to achieve my dream?

What a wonderful opportunity this was for Steve to keep me at his home and in his life. He proposed that I give up my dream of attending Harvard. If I would just stay in Minneapolis for the full four years of my college education, he would set me up in my own apartment in one of his rental dwellings, rent free. No, I insisted. I wanted to go to Harvard, one way or another. To solve my dilemma, Steve suggested I postpone my entrance into Harvard for one year. During that year, I could live at Steve's house and work for him in his businesses, earning enough money to pay for Harvard's steep costs. This plan I agreed to. The effect of this plan was that I took seven years to earn my four year bachelor of arts degree. When I was not at Harvard, I returned to Minnesota to work for Steve.

The summer between high school and what would have been my first year at Harvard, Steve took me on a three-month vacation to Europe. Traveling to Europe had been my long cherished dream. For Steve, it was something he had also wanted to do. How delightful it must have been for him to travel to Europe with his hard-won young man accompanying him. I didn't think of it in the stark terms that actually had developed. But, I had become a male prostitute. I was paying for a very expensive trip with my body and my soul. I was Steve's very own prostitute.

Nevertheless, the trip was a terrific trip. I enjoyed seeing all the sights I had dreamed about as Steve and I drove from place to place in France, Italy, Yugoslavia, Austria, Germany, Belgium, Denmark, and the Netherlands. However, being with Steve for three months, without any respite, I began to see some things I hadn't seen before. Primarily, I saw how often Steve looked for an opportunity to steal or commit a wrong.

In one Paris hotel, while the maids were cleaning rooms, and not watching their linen and supply carts, Steve stole a blanket. I didn't see him do this, but as we drove off from that hotel, one of its monogrammed blankets was in the trunk of our car.

In Copenhagen, Denmark, Steve made a special point of visiting a pornographic bookstore where he bought a deck of playing cards that had printed on them the most disgusting photographs. He insisted on showing them to me. When I was repulsed by them, he downplayed their significance, saying, "These aren't for me. They are for one of my employees back home." Of course, at the time, to bring such pornography back into the United States was quite illegal. That prospect didn't bother Steve a bit.

In Germany, when we asked for some directions from some small town police officers, and they went out of their way to show us what remained of a prisoner of war camp my father had lived in during the last months of World War II, Steve handed me some money and directed that I, in my halting German, offer it to the officers for their kindness. They, thankfully and professionally, refused—no doubt chalking up my crude efforts on Steve's behalf as typically American. I cringed with embarrassment at Steve's crass behavior. We were lucky we weren't arrested for some charge, such as bribing a police officer.

When we visited Amsterdam, the Netherlands, Steve apparently was titillated by the fact that its gay culture was so public. While I was doing some other things, Steve asked around as to where there might be a gay bar, specifically a transvestite bar or cafe. The next day, he insisted on taking me a particular cafe for lunch. Steve spent a lot of time excitedly looking around at the other patrons, but not letting me in on his voyeuristic secret. When we left to return to our hotel, he took great pleasure in telling me every *woman* we saw in that restaurant was a man.

The real test for me happened when we returned to the United States. We landed in New York City and stayed there a couple of days. On the second day, Steve insisted I help him trash our hotel room in such a way as to make it look as if somebody had burglarized it. I resisted. He had never asked me to actively, and *knowingly* participate so directly in one of his schemes. I was being tested. To make a mess of a hotel room was one thing. No crime was committed until the report was made to a third party. Of course, he then demanded that *I* go down to the front desk to report the alleged crime to the hotel staff. Based upon *my* report and the condition of the hotel room, Steve later filed a claim with his homeowner's insurance company for the supposed loss of a valuable camera, some jewelry, and some valuable clothes. When I resisted, Steve told me something I would hear many times during the next few years, "Don't worry. Nothing is going to happen. If anything happens, I'll take full responsibility. So just do as I ask."

As the years passed, prior to my entering law school, Steve involved me in greater and greater schemes. He had me assist him in staging a burglary of his home or his business. I balked at doing so. He repeated his assurances, "Don't worry. Nothing is going to happen. If anything happens, I'll take full responsibility. So just do as I ask." I reluctantly went along. But, more and more, his insistence, and my timid acquiescence to Steve's schemes, began to grow and fester within me. The more I resisted, the more domineering he became. Ultimately, I went along. Had I been caught, I could only have offered the mealy mouthed defense of so many Nazis during the Nuremberg War Crime Trials, "I was just following orders."

The very worst incident happened during the summer between my junior and senior years at Harvard. My junior year had ended, and I visited the National Archives in Washington, D.C., to research a lengthy paper I was planning to write during my senior year. I called Steve long distance from Washington to tell him how long I expected my library research to take, and when I expected to fly home to Minnesota. Steve's voice was desperate. "You have to drop everything and come home right away!"

"If I come home now, I will have to abandon my research for my senior paper. What is so urgent that you need me at home so soon?" I asked.

"I can't talk about it on the telephone. Just come home, now. When is the soonest you can fly home?" he demanded.

"I will fly out tomorrow, if you insist," I answered.

"Good, I will be waiting at the Minneapolis airport to pick you up. Hurry!" he commanded.

In this caper, Steve improvised on his usual criminal routine. He intended to double his profit. He wanted to eat his cake and have it too.

Steve had a forty-foot yacht powered by two engines that needed either to be overhauled or replaced. He compared the engine specifications of the marine engines with those of two aging Lincoln Continentals he owned. He felt, with some slight modifications, he could take the engines out of his two cars and use them as economical replacements for his marine engines.

He hired a mechanic in a garage across town to take the two automotive engines out of his Lincoln Continentals. Steve then took the useless cars to a scrap metal recycler where they were shredded, compacted, and sent off to a smelter in another state. After waiting for a couple months, Steve then put in a claim to his insurance company for two stolen cars.

For some time, an alert police detective had been regularly checking up on Steve and his schemes. The police detective happened to drop by the garage that was storing Steve's two automobile engines. The garage owner told him, "Yes, those two engines are Steve's." The detective put two and two together. Before the detective could obtain a warrant to seize the engines as evidence of insurance fraud arising from the *stolen* Lincoln Continentals, Steve hurriedly picked up the engines and hid them in at a friend's home. Having lost critical evidence against Steve, the detective closely watched Steve. Assuming Steve's own mechanics knew what Steve was doing, the detective came by Steve's service station and garage daily to question each employee, especially the mechanics. But, these employees and mechanics had no idea what Steve was scheming. They also had no knowledge of the two Lincoln Continental engines' whereabouts.

You might say I was the contract hit man called in from out of town to finish some of Steve's unfinished business. When I arrived from Washington, Steve brought me home, told me to put on some work clothes, handed me a toolbox full of wrenches, screwdrivers, and a sledge hammer and drove me to his friend's house. In his friend's garage were two Lincoln Continental engines. At Steve's insistence, I spent a couple days dismantling them bolt by bolt, cylinder by cylinder. In the end, there were two piles of engine parts.

Next Steve instructed me to rent a van from a rental agency. He told me to write a check from my own checking account for the rental, for which he would later reimburse me. I did as I was told, good little Nazi that I was. With Steve's help, I then loaded up the piles of engine parts and two engine blocks into the rented van. Soon thereafter, Steve and I drove the van out into the countryside. As Steve drove the van along country roads, I pitched engine parts out the window into the ditch. When it came to the engine blocks, Steve found a dirt road into an isolated grove of trees a quarter mile from the main road. There we dumped the engine blocks. Throughout the whole affair, when I raised my concerns about the propriety of what I was being asked to do, Steve repeated his mantra, "Don't worry. Nothing will happen. If anything does happen, I will take full responsibility."

At the time, I was twenty-four years old. I certainly couldn't claim innocence of *any* understanding of the matter. However, it took me many years after the fact to piece together all the parts of Steve's plan. The most disturbing facts that finally dawned upon me were these: My fingerprints were on many of the engine parts; the van was rented in my name; and the check paying for the van rental was from my checking account. How would Steve protect me from arrest and trial? How would *he* take full responsibility when the evidence, according to Steve's plan, implicated *me*? While *I* loyally did Steve's bidding, Steve had set *me* up for a fall!

After the evidence was destroyed and disbursed into the countryside, the police detective still dogged the case. He came to Steve's house a few times because he had a few questions for Steve. At one point, seeing the detective at the front door, Steve told me to answer the door and tell the detective Steve was not at home. I did so. Steve, meanwhile, ducked into his bedroom. After the detective left, I went into the bedroom to tell Steve he could come out now. But where was he? The bedroom was empty. I then opened the bedroom closet doors. There was Steve, an adult, forty-eight-year-old man, hiding and cowering in the closet. How could *this* man take responsibility for anything?

Almost a year later, I finished up my last year at Harvard. I thought about what I could do after graduation. Many of my friends were going on to graduate school. Some were going to Washington to intern in government offices. Some were going to Wall Street. The more daring of my classmates were going on lengthy trips to Europe, Africa, or Asia. Some were joining the Peace Corps. The world was theirs for the taking.

As I approached graduation, I did not even consider all the marvelous possibilities then open to me. Incredibly, my mind could only entertain two career choices. I could return to Minnesota and sell used cars with Steve, a prospect guaranteed to be rife with Steve's chicanery, or, I could return to Minnesota to attend law school. Both choices entailed my continuing to live at Steve's house and working for him. Given these choices, after working for several years at Steve's service station and garage, and after participating in Steve's engine destruction debacle, I had the maturity and brilliance to choose law school.

Choosing law school was an amazing choice because over the years Steve repeatedly told me I would never be a very good lawyer because *I did not have the ability to think on my feet.* For Steve, the ability to think on one's feet meant keeping a straight face while you manufacture enough lies to overwhelm your opponents. Steve was right, I didn't have *that* ability, or *that* desire, to quickly and deftly lie through my teeth. Steve was completely wrong, however, about how such skills as he possessed would lead to success in the legal profession.

After graduating from Harvard, I returned to Minnesota. I worked for Steve that summer. During that summer I was given a great gift. At one point during that summer, Steve needed an electrical circuit breaker panel for a small apartment building he owned. He did not want to buy a new one. So, Steve and I drove to a salvage yard we had often patronized when renovating apartment buildings. While there, Steve talked with the owner and asked what used electrical panels he had. The owner told him, "Over in that shed, I have two you might be interested in. The smaller one will cost you *forty* bucks. The larger one will cost you *fifty*." Steve went over to that shed and came back with an electrical panel box and placed it in the van. Steve told me it was the smaller, cheaper box, the *forty* dollar box. While he was gone, I saw an old push broom and a large coal shovel that I needed for a clean up project at a rental property. I put these in the van, also. After a small delay, I followed Steve into the salvage yard office, where the owner was collecting *fifty* bucks from Steve. I assumed the *fifty* buck charge covered the smaller of the two boxes, *plus* the push broom and the coal shovel. But, I didn't speak up to point out I had placed the broom and the shovel in the van. Steve paid the bill, not disputing the issue of *forty* versus *fifty* dollars. We walked out to the van. Steve took the driver's seat. I got in the back of the van.

A moment later, the salvage yard owner, came running out to the van. He threw open the back doors, reclaimed the broom and coal shovel. While doing so, in the loudest and most damning voice possible, spoken more for the benefit of the other patrons walking about the salvage yard, he looked me in the eyes from a few feet away and bellowed, "You God-damned thief! Who do you think you are? You were going to leave without paying for these two tools!" He then slammed the doors in my face, before I could explain.

Steve started the van. He drove out of the salvage yard and we headed home. Meanwhile, I sat in the back of the van, utterly destroyed and completely humiliated. I sobbed and sobbed all the way home. I had not intended to shoplift. But, on the other hand, I had *not* spoken up to clarify the situation when I should have. I was guilty of the theft of an old, used push broom and a coal shovel! Their retail value couldn't have exceeded three or four dollars. Their minimal value couldn't conceal, or redeem me from the fact that I, a twenty-five-year-old Harvard graduate who was about to enter law school, was a common shoplifter.

My humiliation and shame over this incident was unfathomable. As I cried and sobbed to near exhaustion, I realized Steve didn't speak up at all. Over the years, this man had enlisted my grudging assistance in several complicated insurance frauds and other criminal schemes. He had always said, "Don't worry. Nothing will happen. If anything does happen, I'll take responsibility." Well, the fact was, *he* never could have absolved *me* by taking responsibility. Only *I* could be responsible for *my* actions. And in this case, failing to do so, *I* was hopelessly guilty.

I was never arrested or charged for that crime, or for any other crime. But that grisly old salvage yard owner did me a tremendous favor. He shattered my illusions and pierced my state of denial. I always thought of myself as the honest person that lost the third grade spelling bee so many years before. Yet, I could now see the pathetic creature I had become!

That fall, I started law school at Hamline University School of Law in St. Paul, Minnesota. The first year course of study in law school was pretty much the same from law school to law school throughout the country. Lawyers in training need to learn about contracts, torts, constitutional law, civil procedure, property law, and criminal law. In my criminal law class, I was given two great blessings—a mentor and a pamphlet. I met, and, in the course of law school, became the protege of my law professor, Richard T. Oakes. In his class, we were assigned a large criminal law textbook and a small twenty-page pamphlet containing the criminal statutes of Minnesota.

The more we read and discussed the cases in the textbook, and, more importantly, the more we read from the Minnesota criminal statutes pamphlet, I realized just exactly which, and how many crimes Steve had engaged me over the years since I was twelve years old. One day, I sat down in private and started to add up all the years in jail to which I could have been sentenced had I been caught, tried, and held accountable. I was dumbfounded!

Steve had locked me in an emotional and psychological prison since I was twelve years old. I now realized that all of Steve's soothing promises about protecting me from legal responsibility were worthless. I realized, if I continued to do Steve's bidding, I would end up in a real prison, with real bars, real guards, and surrounded by real barbed wire. Also, the only lawyer I would become would be a jail-house lawyer.

I found myself thanking God for sending me a push broom, a coal shovel, and a cantankerous, indignant, old, salvage yard proprietor. I vowed to change.

Towards the end of my first year in law school, the local police detective who had come so close to nabbing Steve regarding the two Lincoln Continental engines continued to inquire into Steve's doings. He discovered Steve sold more than six cars every year. Minnesota law required a person selling so many cars to comply with certain requirements to formally become a car dealer. One of the license requirements was that if you leased your business premises, you had to produce a copy of the lease and some sort of written approval and consent from the landowner. Somehow, Steve managed to get a letter written by the landowner that, Steve felt, met this requirement. To give added weight to the letter, Steve felt the property owner's signature needed to be notarized. I was a notary. Steve presented this letter to me and told me to notarize it. Since the landowner lived in Milwaukee, Wisconsin, and had not signed the letter in my presence, I took my first baby-step towards personal liberation and salvation. I told Steve, "No."

From my criminal law class I learned that notarizing a document without the signer being present was a criminal offense. I was not going to assist Steve in any matter that I might become criminally liable. Steve fussed and fumed. He tried to argue with me. That didn't work. He then decided to punish me with silence. First, however, he said dismissively, "Don't bother. I'll just get my secretary to notarize the letter."

His secretary did go along with Steve's demands, no doubt, because he assured her there would be no trouble and he would take responsibility if any problems arose. A few days later, I pulled out my little pamphlet of Minnesota criminal statutes and read her the appropriate statute, along with the sentence to be served upon conviction. What I said made her extremely nervous. But she really became concerned when the local police detective started calling her to inquire about whether the signer of the letter had *actually* signed it in her presence as a notary. She came within a hair's breadth of being charged with a crime, simply for trusting Steve and for doing his bidding.

CHAPTER THIRTEEN

I Had Enough

Many years ago, in 1973, some bank robbers entered a bank, in Stockholm, Sweden, announced their intention to rob the bank, and took several people hostage. The inevitable standoff developed between the robbers and the police. This standoff lasted several days. The hostages endured incredible strain and abuse. Remarkably, in the course of the ordeal, the hostages became emotionally attached to the robbers. When the hostages were rescued by the police, several of the hostages were *sympathetic* to the *plight* of the bank robbers. This syndrome in which the victim sympathizes with the abuser was termed Stockholm Syndrome by a criminologist and psychiatrist, Nils Bejerot. For many years, I sympathized with Steve and his endless stories and situations of his own making wherein the world marshaled its forces against him. The Stockholm Syndrome applied to me.

Early on, I fought his advances and his influence for a time, as was evidenced by my hiding from him when he came over to our home, or by my defiantly choosing to walk home from twenty miles out in the country. At one point in the eighth or ninth grade, I even tried to sit down with him *man-to-man* to tell him that his and my *friendship* could not continue. His skillful response was to lobby my parents and enlist the help of my older brother in such a way that I finally gave in and returned to his *friendship*.

In those sad circumstances, in order to *get* along, I had to *go* along. And go along, I did. Steve seemingly became my friend, teacher, employer, and mentor while, at the same time, he was my abuser and my torturer.

When I was twelve years old, he was more than three times my age. He was also three times my weight. He was, as a former weight lifter, easily three times as strong as I was. With all this advantage over me, he often wrestled with me. Supposedly, this was just horsing around. But, actually its purpose was to subdue me. He took my arm, bent it behind my back, and pushed it upwards until I screamed with pain and finally yielded to whatever proposition he was advancing. Sometimes, he grabbed my finger, or my thumb, and bent it back until I screamed with pain. Other times, he pinched the tendons and muscles running between my neck and my shoulder. He pinched so hard, I dropped to my knees in submission. One of the most painful things he did to me often occurred during one of our many trips in his Lincoln Continental, during which I spent hours of time with him. He, from the driver's seat, reached over to me with his right hand and pinched the muscles on the inside of my upper left thigh. He squeezed very hard until I gave into his argument or agreed to his plan, whatever it was.

One thing he did to me was particularly outrageous. Steve had a very large boxer dog named King. (As I write this, I realize it had to be a very large dog, a boxer, which might strike fear in others. For Steve, it couldn't have been a yippy little terrier or toy poodle that he owned.) Often, King escaped the house or back yard and ran about the neighborhood. Steve got into his Lincoln Continental and patrolled the neighborhood to find his dog. Sometimes, King engaged in a fight with other dogs, or so Steve told me. In order to break up the fight between King and the other dogs in the neighborhood, Steve purchased a high voltage, electric cattle prod that was powered by five or six D-cell batteries. He supposedly used this cattle prod on King and the other dogs.

A jolt of several thousand volts of electricity certainly catches a dog's attention—and a boy's. On numerous occasions during my teenage years, Steve used this electric cattle prod on me. It was, as so many of his physically abusive tactics were, used in the context of *horsing around.*

Steve's physical teasing, I came to realize, was not a great leap from the Jefferson-99 game inflicted upon me, not my older brothers. It was couched in terms of roughhousing and play, but its real purpose was domination over me. Its primary lesson was *Don't mess with Steve, because, one way or another, Steve won.*

More than forty years later, I discussed with my psychologist this cattle prod and its use against me. For more than four decades, I have mistakenly thought about this cattle prod and the thousands of volts it discharged into my teenaged body in the context of play, of wrestling, fooling around, teasing, and horseplay. It was never play. It was Steve's delight in inflicting pain upon me. It was sadistic torture. My therapist asked me one simple question to burst my long held state of denial and prove the point. I had to honestly answer the question in the negative. "Mark, did you ever see Steve use the cattle prod on his dog, King?"

Steve re-enforced his message with his physical torture and domination of me, particularly when I was a young teenager. As I got older, he reinforced his message verbally. For instance, he often said he knew a man, who for a small fee, would kill anybody Steve chose, and that Steve would never be connected to the murder. Steve's ongoing, implicit and explicit, message to me over the years was, "Don't mess with me! I never get mad. I get even."

As I got older, and physically stronger, the physical domination of me by various means diminished. Yet, he still needed to control me. One trick he resorted to was sleep torture.

When I first moved into Steve's home, I had a small bedroom for my own use. Over the years, and in my intermittent absence from Minneapolis while I was away at college, Steve found other uses for that bedroom as a basement storage area. As a result, and because he rented out the entire second floor to other people, I ended up sharing a bedroom with him.

During the years I worked for him, Steve expanded the persistent line of questioning he used while we drove about in his Lincoln Continental. He expanded his questioning into the middle of the night. Sitting up on the edge of his twin bed, he often awakened me at all hours of the night. He asked me manipulative questions that placed me on the horns of a dilemma. In my half-awake, half-asleep state, he varied the question of earlier years, "Who do you love more, your mother or your father?" Now, he asked, "Who do you care for more, your parents or me?" I tried to give a coherent answer, but I then tried to turn over and go back to sleep. He, in turn, jabbed me in the back with his hand, to reawaken me. He continued his line of questioning. With each attempt to dodge his questioning, by my trying to go back to sleep, he awakened me again. He told me, "I can tell by your conduct, what your real answer is, because your actions speak louder than your words. So why don't you simply tell me the truth." This interrogation went on for hours, sometimes right up until the alarm rang. At that point, exhausted, I got up and went work at his business. The next night, the same routine resumed.

I don't recall how or when it started, but somewhere over the years, I was further manipulated with this sleep torture, and I was given some reprieve, if I engaged in sex with Steve. I could end the interrogation and go back to sleep, if I would prove my love and my loyalty to Steve by engaging in sexual relations with him. This became a habit created and manipulated by Steve. The more often he disturbed my sleep, the more often he engaged me with sex.

I returned to Minnesota after I graduated from Harvard to attend law school in St. Paul. Foolishly, I returned to live at Steve's house. During the first month of law school, Steve continued his late night interrogations of me. I could not cope with the weight of my law school studies and my law school classes if Steve continued to do this. Fortunately, one of his tenants who occupied a couple rooms on the second floor of Steve's old mansion recently moved out of her apartment. It had two good sized rooms, a bathroom, and a tiny kitchenette. I used one of the rooms as a quiet place for me to study for my law classes. One night, during one of Steve's middle-of-the-night interrogation sessions, I simply got up out of my twin bed in Steve's bedroom, found the key to the vacant apartment, walked upstairs, and went to sleep. That was the end of our sexual relationship. The sexual relationship began when I was twelve and continued until that year. I was twenty-five years old. Incredibly, I stopped it by simply moving out of his bedroom and into another.

Many years after the fact, I asked my brother, "When did Steve stop having sex with you? Was it because you went away to join the U.S. Navy?"

My brother replied, "Remember the couple years when you and I both lived on the third floor of our home? Before I graduated from high school, I got tired of Steve coming over in the morning, bothering me in my bed before he went into your bedroom to be with you. To put a stop to it, I simply installed a hook-and-eye lock on the inside of my bedroom door, which I locked at night before going to bed."

A simple hook-and-eye, door latch! Why did he merely put it on his bedroom door? Couldn't he have installed it on the door leading from the second floor landing to the third floor stairwell to protect us, both? Why didn't he buy two hook-and-eyes and offer to install one of them on my door?

Why was Steve stopped by an inexpensive item purchased at the local hardware store? Steve was a big enough and strong enough man that he could easily forced open the door. But he would have done some damage to the bedroom door in doing so.

Steve had ready access to our home throughout the day. This was an era in America when people did not lock their doors in our community. In fact, when our family left on vacation, the doors were left unlocked the entire time we were away. Why Steve didn't come back in the middle of the day and remove my brother's lock still amazes me. The latch as a symbol must have been too powerful for Steve. It told him his time with this victim was drawing to a close, and he had to move on to others.

For my brother, just the act of installing the lock was *his* symbol of *his* growing strength and independence. Faced with this, Steve could not be sure how my brother might respond to the issue of continued sexual access being forced.

Several years later, just the simple act of my refusing to submit to Steve's late night interrogations by moving out of his bedroom was *my* symbol of *my* growing strength and independence.

CHAPTER
FOURTEEN

Metamorphosis

No longer was I Steve's sexual plaything. No longer did I allow myself to be physically abused. No longer did I submit to sleep deprivation and his psychological manipulations in the middle of the night. I still continued to live at his home. I still continued to spend time with him. I still worked for him. I still considered him to be part of my extended family. But our relationship was changing.

More and more, in incremental ways I told Steve, "No." No, I wouldn't notarize a document, unless it was done by the book. No, I would not assist him in his frauds. No, I would no longer run myself ragged to get him out of some jam, or to help him put his best foot forward. For instance, once a year, his service station and garage was inspected by the oil company's sales representative and the district sales manager. Steve's best mechanic had a big reputation for his skills in working on imported cars. But these cars often sat on the service station premises for several days to several weeks awaiting special parts to be shipped from overseas. Therefore, the service station lot was jam-packed with cars. In anticipation of the annual inspection, Steve and his entire staff of employees engaged in a massive clean up. When the district sales manager from out of town came by for the company's annual inspection, the property looked unusually spic-and-span. But this necessitated driving or towing fifteen to twenty cars from the service station lot and parking them in a neighboring grocery store lot, or parking the cars on the street. As soon as the inspection was complete, and the oil company officials drove off to inspect another service station, all the cars had to be located and returned to the lot. For six or seven years, I dutifully helped in this annual farce. By the middle of law school, I simply said to Steve, "No. I won't help you anymore in this madness."

I am not sure why Steve kept me around. Increasingly, I became less pliable to his wishes. I refused to join in his chicanery. I no longer had any present utility to him. Was I being kept around for sentimental reasons? Was I like an old horse that should have been sent to his death and made into dog food or glue? Or was I like an old horse you chose not to dispatch, so you put him out to pasture?

No. Steve saw me as an investment. He still felt he could control me sufficiently that when I finally finished law school, graduated, and passed the bar, I would be comfortably in his pocket. He would own me. I would be a tool upon which he could depend to get him out of scrapes. As a lawyer, I could be a force that Steve could direct in the intimidation of others. I didn't realize his motivation at the time. I didn't realize it until some time later.

I was not completely free from his grasp. When not in law school or studying for classes, I still worked for Steve. More and more, I spent time just accompanying him as his driver while he went about his daily business. I continued to be rather passive in many ways, despite my growing resistance to doing anything on Steve's behalf that smacked of illegality. In one regard, our relationship changed in that I became less the loyal subject upon whom Steve would bestow blessings, and more a person who he was callous enough to exploit outright.

In the early seventies, I bought a duplex apartment building. At the time, I had hopes of becoming a real estate mogul. Taking after my parents, I bought a building that had potential value, but because of its bad cosmetic condition, it couldn't sell. I bought it for about $20,000. After reroofing it, and repainting the entire building, inside and out, I was able to sell it a few years later for over $50,000. After paying off the first and second mortgages, as well as a home improvement loan, I cleared about $25,000. A few weeks after I deposited my profits in the bank, Steve approached me. He was having some temporary cash flow problems that would clear up within a few months. Steve needed to borrow $5,000 from me to tide him over.

A few weeks later, he needed an additional several thousand, and still more after that, until I had loaned him $20,000 of my profits. I naively had faith he would pay me back, but I was not sophisticated enough to secure the loans with a mortgage against his valuable home. I did have a minimum of practical legal smarts in that I required Steve to sign promissory notes for the entire $20,000. In time, Steve repaid part of these loans not in cash, but by barter. I received in trade from him his mother's diamond engagement ring and a used Volvo sedan, which became the first car I actually owned in my name.

For years, I drove cars that were always owned and insured in Steve's name. With some of the proceeds from the sale of my duplex, I bought a used Mercedes Benz sedan. It was a beautiful car, but, frankly, it was my feeble attempt to feed my own need for grandiosity. Bathing in grandiosity saved me from facing the grim realities of my life with Steve. Purchased with my money, but still sleepwalking in my trust of Steve, the car was titled and insured in Steve's name. After a year or so of driving this car, I decided to sell it. I bought it for $5,000, and spent some money having it fixed up and repainted. Since the car was in Steve's name, I let him handle the sale. In its improved condition, Steve sold the car for $6,500. He cashed the buyer's certified check, and without apology or explanation, handed me $4,500. I asked, "What about the rest of the money?"

He replied, "My commission and *miscellaneous expenses.*" That was the end of the discussion. I meekly took the $4,500 he handed to me. I thought I was growing up to be Steve's peer. As such, I thought I was worthy of his respect. But, I did not have enough of my own self-respect to command respect in this transaction, or in anything else.

From Steve's perspective, I was what I always was—I existed to suit his whims and his needs. He was no longer screwing me sexually, but he continued to screw me—psychologically and financially.

Strangely, it had not become crystal clear to me I was moving from his inner circle to just being a member of the world he could take advantage of if the opportunity arose. My *father hunger* and the emotional neediness of the imprisoned twelve-year-old within me blinded me from seeing the harsh truth before me. I saw Steve pull some of the same stunts with employees and others. These people worked hard for Steve, or they entrusted money to Steve. Yet, when the final accounting was made by Steve, somehow the figures never worked out in their favor.

I continued to live and work for Steve as I finished my legal education. I continued to live at his home, in a few upstairs rooms. As I was in my final year of law school, just one semester away from graduation, Steve felt I was about to break free from his control. He decided to test my loyalty, and his control over me.

A year or so earlier, a neighbor of Steve's had observed how Steve seemed to be making money in real estate by buying up old properties, rehabilitating them, and reselling them at a profit. Of course, he saw I had done the same thing. The neighbor bought a four-plex apartment building that was in terrible shape and was located in a rough part of town. Steve advised him on some aspects of this purchase, and at one point promised to buy the property from him. There was a lot of bad blood that arose between the neighbor and Steve and me. I was in the midst of it. To settle the dispute, Steve and I bought the property from him. Steve and I had intentions of working on the property. But for one reason and another, the property stood empty for some time. This could not continue.

Using this pretext, Steve demanded I take a leave of absence from law school to attend to this albatross we both now owned. Ostensibly, I was needed to help renovate this four-plex. I dutifully, though reluctantly, complied. I withdrew from law school just a few credits short of graduation. My law school mentor, Professor Richard T. Oakes, wondered *Why, in heaven's name, was Mark abandoning his goal just short of attaining the prize?*

While I was on leave from law school, did Steve and I make a concerted effort to work on the four-plex? No. I spent the entire time away from law school just waiting and asking Steve, "When are we going to get this thing done? Why did you have me withdraw from law school, if we weren't going to do anything about it?"

For me, my status as Steve's pawn was becoming clearer. My growing dissatisfaction with my state of affairs led, however, to some good things. Towards the last year of law school, I began to examine my life.

One thing that was missing from my life was a girlfriend. As I looked into my future, I wanted to share that future with a wife. Eventually, I wanted to have children with her. I therefore sat down at my desk one day, and started to consider what qualities I wanted in a wife. In observing the world, I had concluded that many marriages struggled because they were entered into without considering what the husband and wife had in common. Love and marriage, for most people, seemed to be a game of chance driven entirely by hormones. I determined to eliminate some of the element of chance. Like Spock in the television show, *Star Trek*, I therefore wrote out some thoughts in a quite dispassionate manner. I refined my list. I then started on a dating campaign. Each woman I dated I compared to my list. If something in her life significantly conflicted with an important point on my list, I tried to reconsider other merits of the person. But, usually I ended up striking her from my list. Thus, if a person was a smoker, she was cut from my prospects. If the person was a heavy drinker, she was cut. If the person was a user of illegal drugs, she was cut. If she had radically different political or religious views than I had, she was cut.

However mechanical or ruthless this process was, it served a redeeming purpose. I was beginning to contemplate a life free from Steve's far reaching control. The imprisoned twelve-year-old boy was emerging from within me. Like a teenager, my adolescence had been subdued, even beaten back. My adolescence was merely delayed. My various struggles with Steve on many planes were, in a sense, teenaged struggles. One of the most telling examples of this adolescent struggle was when Steve and I went grocery shopping. Like a thirteen- or fourteen-year-old boy, I didn't want to be seen shopping with him. On one level it was teenaged rebellion. On another level, I didn't want people to falsely conclude we were a gay couple. On this latter fact, I am sure many people must have mistakenly reached that particular conclusion, quite contrary to my wishes.

At the end of my semester's leave of absence from law school, I returned. I completed my classes and was issued my diploma. I did not enjoy the graduation ceremonies my fellow classmates had the summer before. I graduated in December of 1979 instead of with my class in June 1979. I didn't really care to attend the summer graduation in 1980. I simply went to the law school registrar's office, picked up my diploma, looked at it, and yelled out in disappointment and disgust, "BIG #&!*% DEAL!"

My diploma meant very little if I failed to pass the three-day state bar examination. I signed up for a bar review course, paid my fee, and began studying in the most disciplined manner I had ever studied. I had a little more than a month to relearn and distill the crucial points of the law before sitting for the February 1980 bar examination. Each day, I studied about eight hours. During each of those hours, I sat studying at my desk for fifty minutes, and then took a ten-minute break to stretch, walk around, have a snack, and use the bathroom. Each evening, I attended a session of the bar review course. At the evening session, we listened to lectures or watched videotapes, and practiced writing answers to hypothetical examination questions. When I wasn't studying a book or attending an evening lecture, I listened to audiotapes instructing me further on the crucial information I needed to know to pass the bar. In mid-February, I took the bar examination.

One day, while I was studying for the bar, I telephoned a woman I met a few months before while singing in our church choir. I asked her if she wanted to go out with me that evening. She, to my surprise, agreed. We intended to go ice skating, but ended up going to a bowling alley to bowl a few games instead. Afterward, we went out to dinner. We had a wonderful time. She and her life experience matched my list. I was not threatened by the fact she was a dentist. Throughout the time I studied for the bar examination, we went out several more times. In fairly short order, I fell in love with her. But, she was reluctant. She bode her time. I kept pursuing her. Within a few months, I won her over, and we were planning a future together. More and more, I spent my free time with her. In effect, by April I moved in with her at her apartment although most of my clothes, books, and other stuff remained at Steve's home. I also still picked up my mail at Steve's until mid-summer. By July, I proposed marriage. We set a wedding date for the following April.

During February, March, and April, I awaited the results of my bar examination. While waiting, my life was placed on hold. If I passed the bar, I would be sworn in as a lawyer, and I could begin my legal career. If I failed to pass the bar, I would have to recover from the failure, and begin studying again for the summer bar examination. On the day my notice from the Board of Law Examiners arrived at Steve's home, I was helping a neighbor friend of mine paint one of the rooms of his house. Steve knew how much I anticipated that letter. He came by with the letter for me to read. I opened up the letter. As my disciplined work, and luck, would have it, the letter informed me I passed the bar and would be sworn in as a lawyer in May at the Minnesota State Capitol. Steve left. I immediately called my girlfriend. She came over a little while later to give me a hug and a kiss. She, my neighbor friend, and I opened a bottle of champagne to celebrate my victory.

Steve was happy for my victory. I want to believe, even now, that he was happy for my personal success, and for achieving a long sought goal. But, for him, I think he felt his control over me continued. I think he felt his investment in my becoming a lawyer would soon pay off.

Yet the ground was quaking beneath my feet and Steve's feet. I was spending all of my free time with my girlfriend. I was, for all practical purposes, living at her apartment. Steve was losing control of me. He was losing control to the force that beckoned so many of his past victims—the power of love. Specifically, and antithetically, Steve was losing control to the forces of adult heterosexual love, affirming, life-giving love between me and my girlfriend. Because of his own immature and manipulative psychological and emotional makeup, such a phenomenon was really beyond his comprehension. All he could see was he was losing someone he had controlled for seventeen years. Some years before, Steve commented to me, "Once a young man has sex with a woman, it is like a dog that has had a taste of blood. You can then never again reliably bring the dog to heel." It seemed a crude comment to me at the time. I didn't realize Steve really meant it was a sad occasion for him. He could no longer control his male victims once they fell under love's spell.

In a pathetic and hopeless attempt to destroy this beautiful thing, Steve visited my devoutly religious parents at their suburban home. I had not yet introduced my girlfriend to my parents. Steve asked my parents, "Did you know that your son Mark is living in sin with some woman over in St. Paul?"

Since I was twenty-nine years old, my father replied, "Mark is a free man. He is over twenty-one. He is free to make his own choices and live with the consequences of those choices."

Steve must have felt oddly powerless. He had always been able to manipulate my parents. He had always been able to manipulate me. Was he now losing his touch over both?

Towards the end of May, a very big day in my life arrived. I was sworn in as a lawyer at the Minnesota State Capitol. I promised to protect and defend the constitutions of the United States and the State of Minnesota. As I raised my right hand to give my oath, tears welled up in my eyes. I felt very proud.

In the process, an odd sort of drama played out. My parents, Steve, and my girlfriend were with me that day. I had a relationship with each. Each had control over a part of me. I had many secrets I was keeping from each. How could I ever sort out these relationships and these secrets?

After the swearing in ceremony, my girlfriend returned to her apartment. My parents returned home. I returned home with Steve. Steve had planned a small celebration for me at his home. It was very simple. He and I and his secretary sat on his back deck and each had a slice of some pie and some lemonade. While we were sitting on the back deck, I basking in my new status as a lawyer, Steve announced, "Mark, I have various legal matters I would like you to attend to."

I instinctively knew Steve was collecting what he perceived to be my debt to him. I knew any legal work he would have me do would contain elements of fraud and illegality. I calculated he believed my legal services to him should be free, *after all he had done for me*. I knew from my study of economics, when something is free, people *over* use it and *under* value it. I knew I had worked for Steve for many years on what developed into an unspoken and undefined barter arrangement. I knew I wanted to enter the real adult world. I took a deep breath and said, "Steve, I would be happy to work for you on your legal matters at the rate of seventy-five dollars per hour."

His face flushed red with anger and betrayal. Steve was non-plussed, but tried not to show it.

Later that day, Steve went to my parents' house and complained to my parents. "Do you realize, after all I have done for your son Mark he now had the audacity to charge me for any legal work he does for me?"

My father answered, "Steve, a young man has to make a living."

When Shakespeare's Prince Hal ascended the English throne upon his father's death, and took on the sovereign mantle of state as Henry V, he realized his new office had its own requirements. It could not be tarnished by the continued power and influence of the new king's old drinking buddy Falstaff. When I swore my oath as an attorney, I also realized I had to separate myself from Steve's malevolent power and influence.

At those two respective moments, both Falstaff and Steve felt their respective worlds, collapse in ruin. Henry V would not attain his full powers immediately. Nor would I. But we both were about to embark upon new lives. Our new lives required that we set aside childish things as we learned to become formidable adults.

CHAPTER FIFTEEN

My Emerging Identity

Many people go to law school because they have visions of saving the world. Idealism motivates them. They think a legal education will help them accomplish their grand vision. They soon discover a fly in the ointment. Much of a legal education concerns itself with the details of how a commercial society transacts business, gets paid, and if not paid, what remedies are available short of fisticuffs or gunfire. Thus a law student learns the ins-and-outs of many commercial ideas and procedures, including contracts, sales agreements, deeds, leases, mortgages against real estate, mortgages against personal property, how banks handle checks, and the granting or extending of credit. This very last item seized my attention about half way through law school.

The subject came up in my family law class. In particular, what was a wife to do if her husband is the family breadwinner and she was the housewife and mother? If she were to divorce her husband, would she be able to continue on with life with the same bank accounts and credit card accounts? Would she be a person, for credit granting purposes, in her own right? If she divorced her husband, and the husband remarried, would she, for credit granting purposes, still be the *missus*? Or, would there now be two?

Obviously, Steve and I were not married, and I didn't consider us to be so, in any way. He had, however, made extensive promises to me over the years that since he was a bachelor and had no children, I would be the sole heir to his estate. On this particular point, I later learned he had made the same promise to other young men he sexually abused. This was not my primary concern. What began to concern me was that for years, I worked for Steve, but never received a paycheck. I never paid rent to anyone. I never made a car payment. For my own personal account, I never paid a utility bill. From discussions in my family law courses, I began to wonder, *What was my credit rating? What was my credit profile?*

With respect to a duplex rental dwelling I purchased in the early 1970s, I did have a checking account. I paid for insurance, utilities, and real estate taxes. I paid mortgage payments to a private party. As part of buying the duplex, I legally and formally assumed the obligations of an underlying mortgage on the property. *But, for credit history and scoring purposes, did I exist?*

I decided to test these questions by opening up a department store credit account. I went to one of the downtown Minneapolis department stores. At the age of twenty-six, I obtained an account application and applied for my first credit card. After a week or so, I received a rejection letter. The department store regretted they could not extend me credit because in checking the Minneapolis Credit Bureau records, I did not exist. I was astounded. I lived. I breathed. But to some faceless credit bureau, and one department store, I did not exist.

I went to the Minneapolis Credit Bureau to talk with one of their credit counselors. He told me the same thing, but I could open up a file with the bureau and, in the process, produce whatever evidence of credit history I had. I took the application home and began substantiating my credit life.

But the question haunted me. For the commercial world's purposes, I did not exist. Because of the way I allowed my life to be structured and dominated by Steve, I was a nonperson. I was like the women I read about in family law class whose existence was dependent upon some other person. Since I was just beginning to emerge and struggle against Steve, this judgment of nonexistence was troubling to me.

I began a careful and concerted plan documenting my personal and credit history in order to open a credit bureau file. I then applied for credit cards at various stores and credit card companies. With these new cards, I carefully used them, and responsibly paid my monthly statements on time. I began building my credit history. To the larger world, my existence began to be recognized.

By the end of law school, I used my credit cards more and more. I didn't get into trouble with them by that time. But in using them, I had to pay them with money, just as everybody else in our society had to do. I approached Steve and tried to renegotiate our financial relationship. I needed money to pay my credit cards. Couldn't he pay me a weekly paycheck like he did his other employees? Steve couldn't comprehend my need. On its simplest level, I needed money to pay my bills. On a larger, more important level, I wanted and needed to be respected as an adult in the real world.

Steve responded to my entreaties, "Why do you even need credit cards? I provide you with everything you need: food, transportation, and shelter. Why can't we continue on as we have done so for these many years?"

I needed money to participate in the real world, independently. Not only did I need the coin-of-the-realm to pay my credit card bills, but beginning only a few months after graduating from law school, I needed money to begin repaying my student loans from college and from law school. That was the practical need. But the rub, for Steve, was that I, the young man whose life he had dominated since my early teenaged years, was seeking independence.

Really, as I look back at this struggle, it was a teenager's struggle against a parent. The age old plaintiff cry of a teenager, "Why can't you treat me like an adult? Why do you always treat me as a child?" was echoing in my life. Here I was, a teenager in a body that was approaching thirty years of age.

From my current perspective as a parent, I recognize that even though I struggled with my children while they were growing up, I always held the view they were eventually going to spread their wings and fly from my wife's and my care and shelter. I looked forward to each new advance towards their personal maturity. I often was sad to see one small chapter of their lives come to a close, but I was proud both of our children were taking another step forward in their journeys. Not only was I eager for them to take that next step, but because my wife and I became parents in our late thirties, I was aware that I would not always be around to guide them. Because of this awareness of our mortality, we have encouraged our children to try, even though they might initially fail. If they fail, we have counseled them to step back, reassess their situation, improvise, and try again.

By comparison, Steve, if he ever loved me, never loved me in this manner. Steve always sought to tie and bind me. He always sought dependence and pliability.

Whenever we renewed our discussion about paying me a wage for my labors, we each merely repeated the same arguments. Finally, I lost my temper. We were in the kitchen of his home. I stood up, dramatically knocked over the chair upon which I had been sitting. I then yelled, "Why can't you encourage me in this new phase of my life that I am entering? Why can't you view me as an adult? Why can't you love me like a father?"

Steve sat there with his mouth agape. He thought the temper that I used to display when I was a child and a young teenager had been successfully suppressed by him years before. Here it was re-emerging at the age of twenty-nine. *I* was even surprised at this display. I was surprised I was even having this discussion.

The dependent child argued and struggled with the dominant parental figure. The terms of their relationship had to be reworked and modified if the child was ever to become an adult. But Steve could only thrive when others were dependent upon him. His world was a world where he needed to dominate and control. He could never engage on an adult level with a fully functioning adult. Steve, like Peter Pan, hoped against hope he could keep me in the Land of the Lost Boys. My departure might be delayed, but it could not prevented.

While I awaited my bar examination results, I went out into the world and got a part time job as an assistant to a Minneapolis city councilman. I held this job for about six months. During that time, I received a *real* paycheck, something I had not received since I quit working at the Guthrie Theater so many years before. I was even treated by other adults as an adult. I paid my credit card bills and began paying my student loans.

I still viewed Steve as a member of my extended family. I still, strangely, wanted him to be a part of my life. I just wanted to make a few changes in the way we related to each other. For Steve, however, it became clearer I was no longer within his inner circle. I was no longer a part of a small tribe within which he was the chief. I migrated to the larger world. I became part of the *other*, membership within which placed me beyond the pale. Being part of the *other*, he could continue to exploit me in whatever way he wished, without further pretense of being my friend and father figure.

Within a year or so, whenever I dropped by his place of business, he no longer called me Mark. He began addressing me as Mr. Douglass. In law school, my professors called upon me in class and, out of professional respect, addressed me as Mr. Douglass. Steve now did this, to induce in me feelings of shame and guilt. Steve, by seemingly acting in a polite but distant manner, was using the tool of so many closed communities. In order to discipline me, punish me, and persuade me to return, Steve was, in small, but deliberate ways, shunning me. Steve now called me Mr. Douglass in hopes of securing my capitulation and my return to the fold.

Enduring this form of shunning was painful to me. This shunning, combined with other factors and events, backfired against Steve. My darkened world began to receive flickers of light. The essential goodness and ever-brightening nature of this light eventually banished the evil in my life.

When I was in high school, one of my most beloved teachers, an English and humanities teacher, Miss Westby repeatedly told me, "Mark, remember what the ancient Greeks have told us down through the ages. *Man gains wisdom only through suffering.*"

The early 1980s were a time of great suffering for me. They also were a time in which I gained much wisdom.

CHAPTER SIXTEEN

Wedding

I proposed marriage to my girlfriend in July 1980. I intended to propose to her at Christmastime, but in midsummer we took a trip to San Francisco, California, to visit some college friends of mine. My girlfriend and I had a wonderful time. One day, we drove across the San Francisco Bay bridge to Sausalito. We ate dinner at a lovely seaside restaurant called Ondine's. Our table overlooked San Francisco Bay. As we dined, the moon rose over the bay. We talked about how much fun our trip had been. We talked about our separate hopes and dreams. It just came over me to abandon any plan for a yuletide marriage proposal. No special fanfare, no kneeling down on one knee, not even a diamond ring played a part. I had no rehearsed speech. I don't even recall my exact words. Somehow, in the course of dinner conversation, I threw all caution to the wind, and proposed to her. She accepted. We were both very happy!

From the beginning, we have divided up our world, each taking different tasks. I happen to be somewhat of a dreamer. Thank goodness, my wife is a doer. For instance, on any one evening, I might suggest we go out for dinner. Having formulated the proposition, the idea, or the dream, my mind is content. I am satisfied. My wife, fortunately, engages the proposition and asks about the *details* of its execution. Where shall we dine? When shall we dine? What kind of cuisine did I have a desire for? How expensive a restaurant? Do we need a reservation? Who will make the reservation? Over the years, my wife, more often than not, handled these details. Planning the wedding revealed the same division of labor.

My mind was content with the idea of getting married. Ann executed the details. After a while, Ann was so wrapped up in the details, I became a little angry and jealous I was not consulted in much of anything. In response to my complaint, Ann started to ask my opinion about too many details. Realizing, in fact, I did not really want to do this much planning, and recognizing how Ann was doing such a good job of planning a simple, elegant, somewhat non-traditional wedding, I joked to her, "Just tell me the date and time, and I will show up, showered, shaved, and wearing clean clothes."

Actually, I did have four major concerns. In preparation for our marriage, I wanted us to go through a premarital counseling process called *Prepare*. I wanted a simple, traditional Episcopal wedding ceremony, rather than the write-and-speak-your-own-vows pastoral wedding that was so popular at the time. I also didn't want my mother involved in the wedding planning. Finally, I did not want, what would have normally been expected by my family, Steve as my best man. Apart from these issues, only three of which I voiced, Ann arranged everything else. The result was a lovely wedding and reception at a modest cost.

So many marriages arise from so much focus upon the wedding details. The demands of this ceremonial day often push aside the more important questions, core issues, and compatibilities. The marriage counseling process attempted to address this. Couples undergoing *Prepare* marriage counseling answer numerous questions of an inventory. Actually, they are not so much questions, as statements. Answers to these statements challenge, or at least illuminate, the usual love-smitten belief, "Oh! We just agree on everything!" The topics include communication, conflict resolution, money, leisure, sexual relations, children, family and friends, expected roles, and religious orientation. Answers to the inventory help the marriage counselor lead the couple's inquiry. For instance, if to the statements, *We have a wonderfully satisfying sex life* or *My partner spends money wisely,* one party disagrees, and the other party agrees, there has been a failure to communicate.

Ann's and my *Prepare* inventory highlighted a number of issues. The most important issue noted for me, naturally, was *friends and family*. We discussed some issues with the minister, but we decided I would benefit from some deeper inquiry. The minister gave me a referral to a psychologist he knew.

I called the psychologist and set up an appointment with him. At the appointment, I explained my marriage plans and our premarital counseling with the minister. We talked about some of my struggles with my mother. A bit more than half way through the appointment, I asked, "Are you tape recording this session? (No.) Do you take notes about what is said between us? (Yes, a summary afterwards.) Would you refrain from doing so, if I asked? (Yes.)

I drew a deep breath, thought long and hard, and said, "As you know, I am an attorney. Often when people come to an attorney, they refuse to bring up or address issues of major importance. If the attorney doesn't discover these issues, he might not give appropriate counsel to the client."

The psychologist affirmed me by saying, "The same thing often happens with psychologists and patients. Why do you ask?"

I was committed to marrying my fiancee. I also wanted the psychologist to understand the larger picture in my life. Yet, I feared I might be a homosexual. Nevertheless, I decided to lay my cards on the table. "If you can assure me nothing said in this room today will be repeated to anyone, ever, then there is something you ought to know."

The psychologist said, "Nothing is being taped. Nothing will be written. Nothing will be disclosed to anyone without your written consent and permission."

"There is this close family friend named Steve..." I began. I explained Steve's relationship to our family. I explained my close relationship to Steve. I explained that I lived at his home and worked for him, and we jointly owned a four-plex apartment building. Then, for the first time in the seventeen years, since Steve first molested me, I told another human being I feared I might be homosexual. Whether I was or not, I still feared the world, including my fiancee, might discover my sexual history with Steve.

I feared the psychologist might reply to my vulnerability and my disclosures with, "That is the most disgusting thing I have ever heard in my entire professional life!" He thought pensively for a moment. He probably thought, *This is the first time I have ever counseled a man about childhood sexual abuse! It is a very rare phenomenon. I will have to read up on the matter.* Instead, he responded, "Our time together today is about to draw to a close. Would you like to schedule another appointment?"

I agreed to return in a week's time. As he escorted me to the door, he thanked me for being open with him. He congratulated me for daring to disclose such intimate details. He assured me we would need to discuss things in greater detail at our next session.

We counseled for several months, thereafter. We agreed I should disclose to my fiancee what I could, when I could, but well before the wedding. After a few appointments, I sat down with Ann and said to her, "There is an issue that has come up with my psychologist that we need to talk about." I was still trying to keep my lid on, keep the lid on all the secret details of my relationship with Steve, keep my family's secrets intact, and, in a lawyer-like fashion disclose only as little as I dared to disclose. "At some time in my life, I have engaged in a same-sex relationship. But, at this time, I cannot tell you if it was once, with one man or with an entire regiment of men. I cannot tell you if it was a one night stand, or if it was a lengthy affair. But! I am *not* a homosexual. Can you accept this about me?"

To my great relief, Ann said, "Yes. I love you for who you are. I want to marry you. I want us to be together. If you are able to tell me more someday, I will listen. If you cannot, that will be okay, too." She gave me a hug and a kiss.

In a different, and more profound way, at that moment, I felt happier about Ann's acceptance of me and her love for me than when she said "Yes" to my marriage proposal, or when we both said "I do" at the wedding. I knew I loved this woman more than anyone in the world.

As for the wedding planning, I was greatly relieved that I never had to choose Steve as my best man. Ann decided, and I readily agreed, a simple wedding without a ringbearer, flower girls, bridesmaids, groomsmen, a maid of honor, or a best man would be quite sufficient. Unbeknownst to Ann, failing to choose Steve would have suggested to my parents and siblings something was amiss between Steve and me. To Steve, it would have been a public slap across his face. He had hoodwinked my family for so many years. His charade was so convincing he was named godparent to my oldest brother's son. A few years later, when my next older brother and his wife married in Steve's church, Steve was my brother's best man. Thankfully, Steve would merely be a guest at our wedding.

Early on in the process, I tried my best to maintain a relationship with Steve and my family, as I introduced my fiancee into the mix. These efforts were doomed to failure. I was in deep denial about Steve's and my relationship. Of all of Steve's victims, he deceived and brainwashed me the most successfully, and, seemingly, permanently. Through therapy, I began to realize the pathology of our relationship. With my psychologist's help and guidance, I slowly found small ways to break free from Steve's domination.

Although I began to recognize the wrongful nature of Steve's actions over the years, I was still in very deep denial about how his conduct had harmed me. I still could not discuss with my wife, or my family, the dark secrets of seventeen years of my life. I still remained deeply divided and deeply troubled.

When my wife and I drove about town, we sometimes passed a building, or, as we talked, some thought about past events intruded into my mind. Within a few seconds I changed from being happy and fun to be with, to being sad and troubled. My bride, noting how swiftly an emotional storm had churned my inner seas, asked, "What's wrong, Mark?" Many years later my wife told me when these sea changes occurred, she mistakenly thought to herself, *What have I said or done to cause this sudden change in my husband's mood?* Because so much of me was still imprisoned within me, I could not adequately contend with my stormy seas, nor could I send out a distress call. Although I opened up to my psychologist, and I made a severely limited disclosure to my wife, I could not open up further without blowing my lid off completely.

As for Steve, I continued to speak with him a few times each week, because he still owed me money and because we owned a four-plex apartment building together that we were in the process of renovating. Yet, with my marriage, I was living a new life *without him*. I don't know if he felt like an abandoned spouse, a jilted lover, or if he simply felt, and feared, the pulling and stretching of the shameful mooring lines that still bound us together. For my part, the more aware I became of these tangled mooring lines the more I feared drowning in their web.

No doubt, Steve quietly pondered how he would insure my continued silence as he considered the cards available to him and how he would play them to greatest effect.

CHAPTER SEVENTEEN

Cleansing

Coming from a family of dentists, the joke has always been, since *I* did *not* become a dentist, I married one. Not long after my wife and I married, my father sold his dental practice to her. My wife and I moved from St. Paul to downtown Minneapolis to a small apartment located closer to her new dental office. After living there for several months, a more spacious apartment became available in the same apartment building. We moved to the larger unit, which had a large dining room. After settling in, we decided to do some entertaining of family and friends.

In May 1982, my mother's oldest sister, my Aunt Alice, came to town for a visit. My wife and I decided to host a Mother's Day dinner for her and my parents in our new apartment. Since Steve was considered family, we invited him to this dinner.

My wife prepared a wonderful meal. We all had a good time. The conversation was excellent. Because so many of my elders were present, there were many stories about their youth. Because they saw me grow up, the elders felt compelled to tell amusing stories about my childhood. When it came time for Steve to tell a funny story about me, he decided to preface his story with the following statement, a statement which struck everyone, except me, as a rather leaden one.

Steve boasted with a laugh, "Oh! I know so much about Mark, I could easily blackmail him!" This announcement was immediately followed by his somewhat stilted laughter. Everyone at the table laughed nervously, but their expressions seem to say, *Whatever did Steve mean by that?*

It *was* an odd thing to say, but it had the most specific intention. Steve knew what he was saying. More importantly, *I* knew what *he* was saying. Shocked by this, I don't even remember the subject of his story that immediately followed. What I did know was this: Steve, by jestingly threatening blackmail, was, right then and there, blackmailing me.

The party continued for another hour, before we said our good-byes and our guests departed. I helped my wife clean up. Afterwards, I told her I needed to call my law professor, colleague, friend, and mentor, Dick Oakes. It was not unusual that I called him because we were co-counsel on a couple of legal cases. What might have seemed unusual was that I needed to call him so late in the evening. My wife apparently did not, however, notice anything out of the ordinary.

I told Dick I needed to talk with him the next day about a matter that had come up. He asked me what it was about. Because, I did not want to go into *any* detail, I asked him to hold his questions until our meeting the next day. He understood. We agreed to meet the next morning at the law school.

My wife went to bed. I stayed up for another hour or so contemplating the import of Steve's veiled threats of blackmail. I had disclosed relevant details to my psychologist. I had made the most limited disclosure to my wife. Would I leave things as they were? By doing so, wouldn't Steve have succeeded in silencing me? How do you handle a blackmailer? If you pay a blackmailer or otherwise yield to his demands, can you ever be certain the demands will cease?

The 1960s singer Janis Joplin sang a song that contained a lyric that equated losing everything with the state of being free. I always hated this lyric. It badgered me. That night, Steve embarked upon an express campaign of blackmail against me. He confidently gambled I would be silenced.

What he forgot was, I was the young teenager who, so many years before, was perfectly willing to walk all the way home from Lake Minnetonka, a distance of twenty miles or more, rather than accede to his ultimatums. The battle lines were drawn with that incident so many years ago. It appeared to him he had triumphed over me. I certainly lost many skirmishes with Steve over the years. Now, however, he and I, the forces of good and evil, faced one another in a sort of personal Armageddon—our own Day of Judgment.

I knew Janis Joplin's lyric applied directly to me. I knew the only way to stop this blackmailer cold was for me to lose everything I had ever hoped to hide.

The next day, I kept my appointment with Dick Oakes. He never understood why I withdrew from law school just a semester before graduation. It was also Dick I consulted on a larger matter when I first applied to the Minnesota Board of Law Examiners for permission to take the bar examination. The application to take the examination was rather like a security clearance or a passport application. The board wanted to know the law student's life history, including all of the applicant's wrongdoings. The Board did not want to allow anyone to become a lawyer who was a criminal or who was lacking in *moral turpitude*. I submitted my application completely filled out in exquisite detail, but I did not mention the schemes I participated in under Steve's direction. As a result, my application was, apparently, quite clean.

There was one question on the application, I had difficulty answering. Question twenty-three of my application asked: *Is there any other incident in your career, not hereinbefore referred to, having a bearing upon your character or fitness for admission to the bar?* How could I possibly answer this question in a forthright manner? At the time of my application, I expressed my reservations to Professor Oakes. But I couldn't bring any of the details out in the open. As I hemmed and hawed, Professor Oakes offered, "Mark, everybody has some stupid little things they did as a teenager they are not proud of. You don't really need to explain any of those small transgressions, unless you were arrested, charged, convicted, or formally disciplined in some manner."

At the time, I just couldn't bear to bring up the *stupid little things* I had done. I couldn't bear bringing up the *stupid big things*, either. I said to him, "Okay. Sorry to bother you. I'll answer the question, no."

Almost three years after that halting discussion, I stood before my professor, reminding him of that conversation, and now asked his understanding, his help, and, in a way, his forgiveness for the disclosures I now had to make. If I failed to right this wrong, all Steve would ever have to do would be to pick up the telephone and call the board. An investigation would then be launched, which could end in my disbarment. If I wanted freedom, I had to have nothing left to lose. If disbarment was inevitable, then I might as well face it by my own choice and on my own terms.

Dick Oakes and I spent several months reviewing my entire history. I outlined *everything* I ever did wrong. This was no time for half measures. Full and complete disclosure was required. After sifting through seventeen or eighteen years of my history with Steve, we submitted a six-page amendment to my bar application fully answering its question twenty-three. The amended bar application was then submitted to the Board of Law Examiners for its review.

No doubt, that board was shocked by the extent and the gravity of my disclosures to it. Fortunately, the issue of the sexual abuse of children was just beginning to emerge in the newspapers and television news. Since all my wrongful acts ceased when I began law school several years earlier, and I took major steps to change my life, the board accepted my amendment. In essence, the board told me to *go forth and sin no more*. Dick, as my attorney, was jubilant. He had feared my bar amendment was going to result in the revocation of my license to practice law. I had dodged a bullet, so to speak.

But I saw a greater problem, a turf war between two state agencies charged with the conduct of the legal profession. Up until I was sworn in as a new lawyer, I was under the jurisdiction of the Board of Law Examiners. Once I took the lawyer's oath, I then came under the jurisdiction of a different board, the Board of Professional Responsibility. Being absolved by one board did not relieve me of my duty to face the other board. I knew Steve would continue to have power over my license to practice law until I faced this board also. Dick Oakes did his best to talk me out of making any further disclosures. I dodged one bullet. Why would I want to tempt fate by asking for another?

I thanked Dick for his advice. I told him it was the smart thing to do, and it was the right thing to do. I therefore directed him to present the same facts and the same amendment to the Board of Professional Responsibility, otherwise known as the Lawyer's Board. He reluctantly did so. Once I learned it was in the mail to the Lawyers Board, I knew Steve could do my professional life no harm. What would be, would be—not by Steve's decision, but by my own decision and my own action.

We submitted the entire package to the Lawyer's Board in January 1984. After much delay and much consideration, this board determined

I had not harmed any clients, that the events in question had occurred so many years before, and I was taking steps to change my life. The board, ultimately, did discipline me. Instead of disbarment, I was admonished and placed on a two-year private probation. If I lived up to its conditions, and if I did not engage in any unprofessional conduct, I would emerge with my law license intact. I successfully completed this process in August 1987, and have never been disciplined since.

Protecting my law license was small potatoes compared to the full disclosures I needed to make to my wife and family. Prior to my efforts to save my law license, I had to open up to my wife and my family. In May 1982, a few weeks after the family dinner in which Steve threatened me with blackmail, my wife and I took a weekend trip to an historic hotel in Red Wing, Minnesota. There, I spent the entire weekend telling her the entire story of my life under Steve's domination and influence. It was a long hard weekend. For me, it was like having a dam burst. My outpouring of facts, stories, and tears was, seemingly, endless. My wife accepted me and continued to love me despite seeing an entirely different picture of my life.

In June 1982, I sat down with my parents and made the same revelations. They were devastated. Steve was, in their eyes, a generous and faithful friend. With this new information, they realized Steve was a venomous being, a scorpion. My parents also realized, to some extent, how deeply they failed to protect me from such a creature.

Having made these disclosures to my wife, my family, and to the two state boards, I was free to take on Steve. In January 1984, through the inspired efforts and the representation of my law school classmate, fellow attorney, James W. Kerr, and his law firm, Bergeson, Kerr, Lander, & McDonald, I started a lawsuit against Steve for damages arising from his many years of sexual abuse and torment of me. My lawyers took on my risky case well before the issue of sexual abuse of children became ubiquitous fodder for the news media. The lawsuit lasted for four years. Part of the delay was the normal procedural delays of the law. Some was from Steve's foot dragging. Another part of the delay arose from the fact, I was paying for my legal representation myself. When I had no money, I asked my attorneys to refrain from advancing my case.

Steve would have done better to seek a settlement with me early on, or to seek a court trial early on, because in those four years of delays, the issue of sexual abuse of children, and in particular, the issue of the sexual abuse of boys went from what experts thought to be a rare event, to becoming understood as a widespread societal phenomenon. Thus, when we finally went to trial in May 1988, the jury was already partially persuaded against men such as Steve.

Steve, who had for years, played me as a pawn in his life's crude chess game, and whose silence he thought he had secured through blackmail, now faced my elegantly positioned checkmate!

CHAPTER EIGHTEEN

Trial and Judgment

After several years of delay, my lawsuit against Steve came to trial at the end of May 1988, in Hennepin County, Minnesota. I was represented by my attorney, James W. Kerr. Steve decided to represent himself, although at the end of each day of the trial he went across the street from the courthouse to consult with an attorney about how he should proceed with the next day of the trial. Because I was the plaintiff, my side of the case was presented first. Steve's side of the case was presented next.

The nature of childhood sexual abuse legal cases is filled with proof problems. The molester uses secrecy to commit his crimes. The crimes remain hidden because of shame and guilt, which furthers the secrecy and silence. Usually, there are no photographs, no semen stained clothing or bedsheets, or other physical evidence to prove the case against the molester. The case against a child molester is usually the victim's word against the molester's word.

Juries have the difficult, but human, task of deciding what weight should be given to a witness's testimony. In other words, does the jury believe a witness or not. Often a case succeeds or fails on the believability or credibility of a witness. One of the great tools of a trial lawyer is to catch a witness in a lie. The attorney uses questions, particularly in cross-examination, to snare the witness in inconsistencies and outright lies. This process is called impeaching the witness. If a witness is caught in a lie, even about a small thing, the jury might decide the case in response to the lie, rather than the underlying facts of the case. At a minimum, the lie will cause the jury to discount the witness's testimony. Catching a witness in a big lie usually completely destroys the value of his testimony. It may consequently destroy his entire case, if the witness is a party to the case.

My attorney used the impeachment strategy against Steve on the very first day of trial. My attorney called Steve as the first witness. Steve took the stand and was sworn in by the court reporter. Steve promised to tell the truth when he raised his right hand and gave his oath. My attorney then questioned Steve along these lines.

ATTORNEY: How old are you?

WITNESS: I am sixty years old.

ATTORNEY: Are you married or single?

WITNESS: I am a bachelor.

ATTORNEY: Are you a homosexual?

WITNESS: No.

ATTORNEY: Have you ever had any kind of sexual relations with a man?

WITNESS: No. Never.

ATTORNEY: Are you a pederast or a pedophile?

WITNESS: No. And I object to any suggestion by you or anyone else that I am.

ATTORNEY: Have you ever had any kind of sexual relations with a boy?

WITNESS: No. Of, course not, counselor!

ATTORNEY: Never?

WITNESS: No. Never!

ATTORNEY: Have you ever had any sexual relations with Mr. Douglass?

WITNESS: No. I spent a great deal of time with him. He lived at my home for a time. He worked for me for several years. I was very generous to him. I helped put him through college. But, no. I never had sex with him.

My attorney asked Steve numerous other questions about a great many things, but the above line of questioning at the opening of the trial destroyed Steve's credibility. The destruction was not caused so much by the questions or the answers, but by what followed.

My attorney called, as the next witness in my case, a young man in his twenties who testified at length about how he had come to know Steve, and how Steve went about repeatedly molesting him on numerous occasions beginning at about age twelve or thirteen and continuing throughout his teenaged years. This young man's testimony was followed by that of his younger brother, who testified to the same pattern of molestation. The next witness was my next older brother who testified to the same pattern of abuse.

After that, whatever defense Steve presented to the jury was worthless. The jury members saw he was a liar, through and through. That was enough for them to make their decision against him.

But, other witnesses for my case had to testify. My mother testified about the long term and close relationship Steve had with our family. I testified at great length. My psychiatrist and psychologist testified as experts. They made psychological and economic assessments as to how much my earning ability was damaged because of Steve's abuse.

When we rested our case, Steve presented his case. Since he had no attorney, he gave a general narrative of his long term relationship with me and my family. My attorney just let Steve go on and on. The longer Steve talked, the deeper the hole he dug for himself.

Steve made at least two other major mistakes in this trial. The trial started on a Wednesday before the Memorial Day weekend. The trial could have easily finished by lunchtime on Friday of the holiday weekend. For some purposeful, but unexplained reason, Steve extended his narrative testimony late into the afternoon. It was obvious he was intentionally playing out the clock until the day's end. The effect was that the jury couldn't leave early to get on with their holiday weekend plans. Also the jury was burdened throughout the weekend and the Monday holiday, knowing they had to return to the courthouse on Tuesday to deliberate and decide upon a verdict. I think the longer Steve rambled on, the greater the anger the jury felt for him.

Steve committed another error. Each day of the trial, my attorney and I showed up in the courtroom with three large boxes full of evidence. The boxes were filled with documents, photographs, promissory notes, deeds, and witness deposition transcripts. A trial attorney must be able to swiftly locate important documents in the middle of the trial to present the documents as evidence, or to use some documents to impeach a witness. Steve, on the first day of trial, showed up with only a briefcase full of paper. Looking at our three boxes of evidence, Steve, no doubt feared the *appearance* of his case looked weak. To make a false showing of strength to the jury, Steve made a stupid mistake. Beginning on the second day of trial, Steve arrived with four or five boxes! *He* didn't dolly these boxes in by himself. He had a *young* man in his early twenties dolly these boxes into the courtroom. At the end of each trial day, Steve ordered the same *young* man to pile the boxes up and dolly them out to Steve's car. Throughout the trial this *young* man watched the trial, or waited out in the hall outside the courtroom. The jury took notice...*older* man in the company of a *young* man, many years his junior.

Upon returning from their Memorial Day weekend holiday, the jury deliberated for a few hours and decided in my favor. The jury awarded me a judgment of $1.27 million. About $270,000 of this judgment was for my injuries, expenses, and estimated future lost earnings. Fully one million dollars was awarded to me as punitive damages.

My long journey and struggles had finally come to a triumphant end. Or so I thought.

CHAPTER NINETEEN

Harsh Reality

Fantastic! The jury awarded me over $1,000,000. Following the trial, I was lauded on the local television news. The next day on the front page of the *Minneapolis StarTribune* trumpeted a lead article about my case against Steve and my triumph over him! In the next few weeks, I appeared on a local television talk show. Several weeks later, the nationally syndicated *Sally Jesse Raphael Show* called me, wanting me as a guest on the show. At the time, that nationally syndicated television show reached about seven million people per broadcast. I really felt as though I was in the vanguard of an important issue, namely, allowing childhood sexual abuse victims to sue the perpetrators of their abuse many years after the fact. But after my brief time in the spotlight, the attention and the exhilaration passed. The media turned its focus onto other things. My *fifteen minutes of fame* came to a swift end.

My fame, of course, was ephemeral. Changing the law held more substantial hope for me. But there was no reason for me to appeal my legal victory over Steve. Steve could have appealed his defeat, but chose not to do so. Because neither Steve nor I appealed the legal case, its legal significance was minimal. I had originally hoped to take the case up on appeal to the Minnesota State Supreme Court in hopes of having it repair the Minnesota statute of limitations governing child sexual abuse cases. Having missed this opportunity in my own case, I realized the best approach was to approach the Minnesota State Legislature about the issue. I wrote a letter to the appropriate legislative committee and to the state attorney general's office. In the next year's legislative session, bills were introduced to allow survivors of childhood sexual abuse to sue many years later due to their typically delayed discovery of their injuries. I testified at a couple legislative committee hearings about these bills. Due to my own efforts, but mostly due to the efforts of a great many people, the bills passed into law. I had set out to achieve this result, and I helped achieve it.

But my success was to meet with disappointment once again. A few years later, a childhood sexual abuse, delayed discovery lawsuit went up on appeal. The appellate courts narrowly read the language of the new statute in such a way as to highly restrict its effect and its applicability. The statute was intended to allow lawsuits to begin many years after the sexual abuse at a time when the person fully realized the connection between his various emotional and psychological injuries with the abuse that happened so many years before. The appellate courts decided if a childhood sexual abuse victim showed any guilt, remorse, or any conduct by the child such as his avoiding his molester, then the limited time within which to sue began, rather than being delayed under the new statute of limitations. This decision gutted the new law I helped get on the books.

Since that court decision, bills have been introduced into the Minnesota House and Senate to legislatively overturn the appellate courts' decisions, but the bills have not passed into law. Thus, my hopes were dashed.

To top all of this off, the incredible judgment I was awarded was uncollectable. Rather than appealing the case to a higher court, Steve just hid his money and his assets so that the sheriff, acting on my behalf, could not find and seize them. Since Steve was such a liar, it proved hard to get information from him about his money and his assets' whereabouts. I never collected a dime of the judgment.

On a positive note, the existence of a $1,000,000 judgment against Steve prevented him from borrowing money from banks. It also prevented him from getting a mortgage. As a consequence of this, when his home needed a major roof replacement costing about $15,000, Steve could not obtain a loan to have this work done. As a further consequence, because he was not keeping the building in good shape, his mortgage bank foreclosed his mortgage. Steve lost his home.

On another positive note, whenever Steve tried to submit a claim for damages against his insurance company, whether the claim was real or fraudulent, the insurance company denied it. To the insurance company, the large judgment against him indicated Steve's claims were made because he was in dire financial straits.

Steve's high flying insurance fraud driven lifestyle came to an end. Although Steve was able to swindle a few more people, the world finally proved to be just. Rather like the time during my father's childhood when he bought a new baseball mitt with stolen money and he ended up losing the money and the mitt, the world and circumstances exacted a toll upon Steve.

Steve's health declined. He suffered a major heart attack. He was hospitalized and given heart bypass surgery at our county hospital. Some of the money he had hidden from me went to pay for his hospital bills. A couple years later, in 1992, Steve died of another heart attack while shopping for his weekly groceries. He had been reduced to living life on a strictly cash basis. He was working part time in a menial job and receiving his pay under an assumed name. He had some money in his wallet. He was also collecting welfare benefits. The big man who had a penchant for driving big, expensive cars, living in a large home, and playing with large yachts had been dealt a leveling blow by his own misdeeds and the fates. His body sat in the county morgue for some time. In one good service to mankind, Steve's body was finally donated to the University of Minnesota Medical School for dissection in anatomy class.

A kind hearted cousin of his came into town to wrap up Steve's meager affairs. A short notice was placed in the obituary section of the *Minneapolis StarTribune*. The cousin even scheduled a memorial service. But, because Steve had taken advantage of so many people sexually and financially, it appeared likely no one would even show up for such a memorial service. Therefore, even the memorial service was canceled.

Many years before, while Steve and I were driving around in his Lincoln Continental, Steve spotted a man walking down the street whom he knew. The man looked quite old, crestfallen, and defeated as he walked down the street. Steve said to me, "That man used to be rich. His wife and family loved him. He had many friends. But he lost his money. His wife died. His children grew up and, for reasons of their own, refused to speak with him any more. Even his friends deserted him. God! I hope that never happens to me!" How fitting a similar end befell Steve.

As for me, Steve continued to preoccupy me. I still remained angry and depressed about what he had done to me. My own health suffered. In my late forties I nearly died of a heart attack. I sought medical help and was told I might not live another day, week, or month, unless I submitted to heart bypass surgery. I repeatedly balked at several doctors trying to place me on the horns of a dilemma, as Steve had done so many times before. I therefore refused the surgery and sought other medical, rather than surgical, approaches. This whole experience suggested to me I needed to make changes in my life if I wanted to live to see my children graduate from high school. I am happy to say that changes in my diet and exercise, plus the ingestion of a truckload of pills over the past decade have brought me through that crisis without resorting to surgery. Recent heart research has shown for patients like me, pursuing the medical route is just as effective as choosing the surgical route. I feel good about the health care decisions I have made.

Depression still dogged me, however. At one point, the depression, combined with some bad business decisions, brought so much despair into my life I came very close to committing suicide. One day in my office, I contemplated my circumstances. I sat down at my desk with a pen and a legal notepad. I charted out various paths I might take to address my suicidal despair. I considered the pros and cons of divorce, bankruptcy, closing my law practice, working in some other capacity using my legal education, and suicide.

Providentially, I did not choose to divorce my wife. I did not file for bankruptcy. Most importantly, I did not commit suicide. I started taking anti-depressant medicine. I did choose to close my law practice. I then went to work in the insurance industry helping others fashion their financial and estate plans. I kept my law license. I survived.

I slowly went from being painfully and miserably depressed to moderately happy. Yet, Steve still occupied my thoughts. I couldn't seem to be rid of him. I couldn't place what he did to me in any sort of hopeful perspective. The essence of my problem was I had spent much of my life not following blissful and satisfying endeavors. More importantly, I had spent most of my life seeking happiness from external things and accomplishments. I slowly, in an almost glacial manner, started to conclude there is no reliable happiness in things outside of ourselves. But where could I then find happiness and contentment? If happiness could not be found in external things and accomplishments, where could I find it?

CHAPTER TWENTY

The Source of Happiness

As long as I can remember, I have been a perfectionist. Both my grandmothers were perfectionists. Both my parents were perfectionists. It is fair to say, I come by a good part of it naturally. Part of my perfectionism came from my childhood misinterpretation of one of my Sunday school lessons. We were taught that each and every one of us was *God's perfect child, and that God loved each of us*. I am afraid I twisted these teachings around. I came to believe, *only when I am perfect, will God love me*. A corollary of this that formed in my own mind and heart was no matter what I do, I will never measure up.

When I played with my brothers who were three years and eight years older than I was, I never understood how or why they each could hit a baseball with such skill, shoot a hockey puck so well, or throw a football. Intuitively, I knew I was just as smart as they were, so why couldn't I possess just as much athletic prowess and skill?

During grade school, our report cards were graded simply as *satisfactory* or *needs improvement*. The grades were thus "S" or "N." My report cards were usually filled with many an "S." The few times I received an "N," I felt badly about myself. When I went on to junior high school and high school, I had the same dilemma over letter grades. If I didn't get an "A" or an "A-," I felt badly.

Being the best, or nearly the best, was easily achievable in grade school. It was still achievable in junior high and, less so, in high school. When I went off to college at Harvard, it was not readily achievable by me at all. Likewise, my performance in law school left me sorely lacking in self-esteem.

Of course, the higher I was promoted in school, the harder the competition was. At Harvard, I was surrounded by several thousand young men and women who were just as smart, if not smarter than I was. Most were just as determined, if not more determined than I was.

Dr. Laurence J. Peter's book *The Peter Principle* spelled out a business organization characteristic he observed. "In a hierarchy every employee tends to rise to his level of incompetence." In my climbing the ladder of higher education, the Peter Principle proved true. I was promoted to the level of my incompetence. (To be fair, however, most of my classmates did not carry the emotional and psychological baggage I carried.)

I had engaged myself in a losing game of frustration. I insisted on perfection as being the minimum standard. This inevitably led me to disappointment, self flagellation, and recrimination. At the very heart of things I was unhappy. My unhappiness and discontent were always there. They were clearly made worse by my exposure to Steve. If I carried two pieces of unwanted baggage when I met him, namely my unhappiness and discontent, I became a heavily burdened porter thereafter. I carried the additional bags of shame, guilt, isolation, sadness, and loneliness.

To address my heavily burdened life, I often tried to avoid the *present* pain, by focusing on something outside of myself, usually a *future* goal. When I was enrolled in school, I thought, I will be happy when I finish this homework. I will be happy when I pass that next test. I will be happy when the semester is over...when the school year is over...when I graduate sixth grade...when I graduate from junior high school...high school...college...law school. When I finished school, I thought I will be happy when I pass the bar examination...when I become a lawyer...when I make a lot of money...when I get married...when I free myself from Steve...when I win my lawsuit against Steve...when I get a large jury verdict against Steve... I will be happy when...

At each juncture, I experienced a small amount of satisfaction. The glow soon faded and I was then flooded with dissatisfaction, disappointment, and discontent. To remedy this, I looked to another future event for salvation. Salvation never came for me by this misguided process.

In all these things—accomplishments, diplomas, certificates, status, money—I could never find happiness. Happiness was illusory for me because, I looked for it outside of myself. I remember complaining to one of my first therapists back in the early 1980s, "I don't like the business of legal practice. I have all these money troubles. But, I know I would be happy if I were to make $50,000 a year. Man! Then I would be happy!"

My therapist calmly, wisely, but firmly said to me, "No, Mark. When you are happy, then the career satisfaction and the money will come. But they will come not a moment sooner." It was so axiomatic, I begrudgingly conceded the point to him. Had I paid attention in Sunday school so many years before, I would have taken to heart the lesson found at Luke 17:21 in the Authorized King James Version of the Bible:

> Neither shall they say, Lo here! or, lo there!
> for, behold, the kingdom of God is within you.

I would have realized much sooner that happiness comes from within, not without.

EPILOGUE

In the summer of 2007, our eighty-six-year-old neighbor from across the street died. His name was Logan Coombs. Our family lived across the street from him and his wife, Betty, for nineteen years.

What I admired and envied most about Logan was, more than any other man I have known, his life had a simple harmony and unity to it. Unlike me during my many years as a lawyer, he chose a line of work and stayed with it his entire working life—*because he loved it.* He was a commercial aircraft mechanic and found great joy in his work. Many years ago, I asked him how he chose his life's work. He told me, "I knew when I was ten years old, back in Indiana during the Great Depression, I wanted to work with and be around airplanes." Money or prestige were not issues for him. By following his bliss, as the late author Joseph Campbell advised us all to do, Logan found contentment, a good living, and the respect of his peers. Even in his retirement, Logan worked with airplanes. He combined his lifelong photography hobby with his love of aircraft.

Logan was a proud World War II veteran of the U.S. Army Air Forces. He was buried at the Minneapolis Fort Snelling National Cemetery with military honors. This national cemetery lies right next to the Minneapolis-St. Paul International airport and across the street from the airplane hangars of Logan's former employer, Northwest Airlines. During the funeral ceremonies, we could see and hear the many jet airplanes taking off over us. For many, such a noisy cemetery would not be a desirable place to be buried. For Logan, it was the perfect setting. Logan, in life and in death, exemplified unity and integration.

On the way home from his funeral, I pondered the many soldiers buried in that cemetery. I considered the difficulty many combat veterans have had adjusting to civilian life upon returning from our nation's various wars.

Many combat veterans hide large pieces of their lives from friends and family. These veterans cannot talk about significant aspects of their lives. To avoid dealing with troublesome emotional and psychological issues they downplay or even refuse to discuss their wartime experiences. Only in the company of other combat veterans can they let their memories and their personal demons out into the light. They, of course, struggle to a greater or lesser degree with post traumatic stress disorder, and other psychological and emotional disorders. My father, a World War II B-17 bomber pilot and a prisoner of war, was one such combat veteran. To the degree these veterans wall off one part of their lives from other parts, they are fractured and divided. They are not whole.

Since my neighbor's funeral, I have been making new observations and connections about my own life. My life fractured in 1963 when I was twelve years old. That summer, Steve molested me. By his selfish act, at such a critical time in my development, Steve divided me in two. His crimes against me over the years cut off my emotional and psychological development from my physical development. My body matured as the years passed, but that twelve-year-old boy was scarred and imprisoned by Steve's evil deeds. Each new assault upon my person and my psyche by him further imprisoned me. With each new crime and indignity Steve engaged me in, the entrance to my prison was made more impenetrable. Thus locked in solitary confinement, that child could not easily reunite with the physical and chronological man I am today.

Throughout my teenaged years and my adulthood, I made a great show at achieving various goals and awards. I was an Eagle Scout and a high school honor student. My high school senior class elected me its class president and also voted me "Most Likely to Succeed." I went to Harvard University for college, graduating with departmental honors in history. I captained the varsity rifle team and earned two varsity letters. After college, I attended law school in Minnesota and practiced as a lawyer for more than twenty years. Sadly, these awards and achievements were mere trinkets. Unlike trinkets awarded by the Great Oz to the Lion, the Scarecrow, and the Tinman in Frank Baum's *The Wizard of Oz*, none would give me true courage, an insightful mind, or a caring heart. My achievements were hollow substitutes for the integrated life I lacked. Achieving my goals and becoming a lawyer may have been my way of donning a persona, which compensated for my lack of personal integration. But this persona was not genuine. I was largely a costumed impostor. Becoming a lawyer allowed me to show a seemingly powerful, manly self to the world, even though I could never truly be alive and potent so long as my twelve-year-old self remained locked up.

Abraham Lincoln in his 1858 senate campaign against Stephen Douglas said, "A house divided against itself cannot stand!" He was talking about our nation: half slave, half free. That nation would be made whole only by a bloody struggle, our Civil War. Lincoln's quote was also apropos to my life. I was divided. A great deal of my personal energy went into shoring up my divided and fractured self. The surest example of this was my ongoing battle with depression that started when I was a teenager. Usually it was a low-grade depression known as dysthymia. However, every few years, my dysthymia regressed into major depression. The siren song of suicide often tempted me with salvation from my pain.

In my adulthood, and beginning in 1980, I sought psychological help. Over the years I battled depression, but often, once I emerged from crisis, I discontinued my counseling sessions. No crisis; no need for counseling. Sometimes, I ended my therapy because of financial concerns. I didn't have enough money to continue on with my therapy. Therapy was not as pressing an issue as other more pedestrian demands on my life and my resources.

By analogy, it was as if my car tire had a slow leak. When I was able by my own means and choice, I monitored the tire pressure level. Every so often, I would go to the service station to add air to the tire. But when I descended into crisis mode, I was unable to continue monitoring the air pressure. The tire would go completely flat. At these times, I would call upon the emergency roadside repair service, *my therapists*, to rescue me by putting some more air in my tire. They would tell me, "You really need to spend the extra money and take the time to discover the source of the slow leak."

I would pay them their fee and say, "No thanks. I don't have time right now. See you later." This attitude worked with other factors to my detriment. I never got to the heart of my troubles. I never embarked upon a concentrated and committed therapeutic program.

Over the years, I had six therapists, for whose help I am grateful. They helped me survive. In the decades before the Amsterdam shooting incident, I engaged five. The first moved his office across town far enough away, I did not want to commute to it. The second died. His partner and co-therapist closed their practice. The fourth also closed his practice and moved to his wife's home country, Canada.

The fifth counseled me to give up my law practice to become a laborer. He thought this would help me understand I was a human "being" of value, and not a human "doing," whose value was dependent upon accomplishments alone. This therapist's prescription would have been the perfect cure for me. But, at the time, I found it too bitter a pill to swallow.

I discontinued my therapy with him, although, ultimately, I did quit practicing law. In doing so, I eventually realized the wisdom of his advice.

Returning to the tire analogy, the shooting in Amsterdam was a blowout for me. There was no question that incident destroyed my previously leaky tire. I was not going to drive my life's car any further without professional help and a new tire. Thus, I sought and found my current therapist. Together, we worked through the Amsterdam shooting incident and its ramifications. We then went on a great archaeological dig in which we excavated and re-examined my experience as a childhood victim of sexual abuse. The difference this time was I was motivated and committed to changing my life.

You see, the gunman's volley of five or six shots, one of which came close to killing me and my daughter, was a great gift. Being in my mid-fifties, I was becoming vaguely aware of my mortality. The shooting and my resultant PTSD made me acutely aware of life's fragility. If I were ever to resolve the issues of my childhood, now was the time. I knew I had to uncover that twelve-year-old child, bring him into this world, and unite him with my fifty-plus-year-old body and mind.

I had much help over the years from my therapists, friends, colleagues, and, most of all, from my wife. But the decision and the resolve to finally change had to be *my* decision and *my* resolve.

On that lovely spring day in March 2004, on the edge of Amsterdam's Vondelpark, an unknown sociopath toting a .45 caliber Thompson submachine gun fired his gun in our direction threatening me and my twelve-year-old daughter. In doing so, he inadvertently handed me a key to freedom and a renewed life—an integrated, whole life. But, *I* had to insert the key and turn it to unlock my prison cell to set my twelve-year-old self free.

Who will hand you the key to your childhood's prison cell?

Will you insert that key into your cell's lock? Will you choose to turn the key? If you need a little help turning the key and opening the cell door, will you seek help?

I hope and pray that you will so you can begin living your life to its fullest joy. I can tell you it is worth the effort. You have nothing to lose but the prospect of regaining the freedom that was taken from you so long ago. You have everything to gain in a renewed and vital life focused on the present and future rather than on the past.

You deserve a better life. Reclaim yours and see for yourself. Turn the key. Unlock the cell door. Step out into the bright, warm, life giving light of day.